GRAMMAR

Alexandra Green

World Wonders 4 Grammar
Alexandra Green

Publisher: Jason Mann
Director of Content Development: Sarah Bideleux
Associate Development Editor: Kaye Lafyati
Art Director/Cover designer: Natasa Arsenidou
Text Designer: Tania Diakaki
Compositor: Nora Spiliopoulou
National Geographic Editorial Liaison: Leila Hishmeh

Acknowledgements

Illustrated by Panagiotis Angeletakis, George Melissaropoulos

We are grateful to the following for permission to reproduce copyright photographs:
Richard Nowitz/National Geographic, Greg Dale/National Geographic, Alaska Stock Images/National Geographic, Justin Guariglia/National Geographic, Alaska Stock Images/National Geographic, Kenneth Garrett/National Geographic

© 2011 New Editions, a part of Cengage Learning

ALL RIGHTS RESERVED. No part of this work covered by the copyright herein may be reproduced, transmitted, stored, or used in any form or by any means graphic, electronic, or mechanical, including but not limited to photocopying, recording, scanning, digitizing, taping, Web distribution, information networks, or information storage and retrieval systems, without the prior written permission of the publisher.

For permission to use material from this text or product, submit all requests online at www.cengage.com/permissions
Further permissions questions can be emailed to
permissionrequest@cengage.com

World Wonders 4 Grammar Student's Book
ISBN: 978-1-111-21823-2

Cengage Learning EMEA
Cheriton House
North Way
Andover
Hampshire
SP10 5BE
United Kingdom

Cengage Learning is a leading provider of customized learning solutions with office locations around the globe, including Singapore, the United Kingdom, Australia, Mexico, Brazil and Japan. Locate your local office at:
international.cengage.com/region

Cengage Learning products are represented in Canada by Nelson Education, Ltd.

Visit Heinle online at **elt.heinle.com**
Visit our corporate website at **www.cengage.com**

Printed in Greece by Bakis AEBE
2 3 4 5 6 7 14 13 12 11

Contents

Introduction to World Wonders		4
Introduction	Countable & Uncountable Nouns, Describing Quantities, Parts of Speech & Confusing Words	5
Unit 1		
Lesson 1	Present Simple & Present Continuous	8
Lesson 2	Stative Verbs	12
Lesson 3	Direct & Indirect Objects	15
Unit 2		
Lesson 1	Past Simple & Past Continuous	18
Lesson 2	Used to & Would	23
Lesson 3	Used to, Get used to & Be used to	26
Review 1		30
Unit 3		
Lesson 1	Present Perfect Simple, Present Perfect Continuous & Present Perfect Simple vs Present Perfect Continuous	33
Lesson 2	Relative Clauses	37
Lesson 3	Too & Enough	41
Unit 4		
Lesson 1	Past Perfect Continuous	44
Lesson 2	Past Perfect Simple & Past Perfect Simple vs Past Perfect Continuous	47
Lesson 3	Articles	50
Review 2		53
Unit 5		
Lesson 1	Future Simple & Be going to & Future Continuous	56
Lesson 2	Future Perfect Simple & Future Perfect Continuous	60
Lesson 3	Present Tenses (future meaning) & Future Tenses	64
Unit 6		
Lesson 1	Modals 1: Can, Could, Be able to, Would, Have to, Must & Needn't	68
Lesson 2	Modals 2: May, Might, Should & Ought to	73
Lesson 3	Modal Perfect Forms	76
Review 3		79
Unit 7		
Lesson 1	Zero Conditional, First Conditional & Second Conditional	82
Lesson 2	Third Conditional, Wish & If only	86
Lesson 3	Conditionals with Modal Verbs	90
Unit 8		
Lesson 1	Gerunds & Infinitives	93
Lesson 2	Clauses of Purpose	97
Lesson 3	Causative	100
Review 4		103
Unit 9		
Lesson 1	Reported Speech: Statements	106
Lesson 2	Reported Speech: Questions, Commands & Requests	110
Lesson 3	Reporting Verbs	115
Unit 10		
Lesson 1	Passive Voice: Present, Past & Future	119
Lesson 2	Passive Voice: Gerunds, Infinitives & Modals	123
Lesson 3	Linking Words: Even though, Although, Despite, In spite of, However & Whereas	126
Review 5		129
Unit 11		
Lesson 1	Adjectives & Comparison of Adjectives	132
Lesson 2	Adverbs of Manner, Place, Time, Degree & Comparison of Adverbs	136
Lesson 3	Adjectives ending in -ing/-ed, Adjectives & Infinitives	140
Unit 12		
Lesson 1	Pronouns: Reflexive, Indefinite & Possessive	143
Lesson 2	Review of Tenses	147
Lesson 3	So & Such	153
Review 6		156
Irregular Verbs		159
Word list		160

Introduction to World Wonders Grammar

Welcome to *World Wonders Grammar*, a four-level grammar course that has been designed to cover the needs of students at beginner to intermediate levels. *World Wonders 4 Grammar* accompanies *World Wonders 4 Student's Book*. Each unit in *World Wonders 4 Grammar* has three lessons which correspond to Lessons 1, 2 and 4 of *Word Wonders Student's Book*. *World Wonders 4 Grammar* can also be used with any other intermediate course.

World Wonders 4 Grammar Student's Book

The student's book consists of an introduction, twelve units and six reviews. Each unit contains three lessons. The wide variety of task types, including picture-based and photo-based tasks, will keep students motivated and help them to grasp the grammar points easily. The book is of a manageable length and can be completed in one school year. The amount of time spent on individual grammar points will largely depend on teaching situations and the ability of the students.

Each lesson begins with a cartoon presentation designed to introduce the grammar in an amusing way. This is followed by grammar theory with example sentences. *Remember!* boxes appear often and serve to remind students of things they should be aware of. The lesson then continues with a selection of graded grammar tasks before finishing with the speaking task. The speaking tasks have been carefully written to encourage students to practise the grammar points they have just learnt in realistic situations.

There is a review after every two units of *World Wonders 4 Grammar*. Each review contains a variety of tasks designed to consolidate the grammar covered in the preceding two units. The review ends with a non-fiction Writing Project featuring National Geographic photography. Students then have the opportunity to do their own Writing Project.

At the back of the book there is an alphabetical word list of key vocabulary for each lesson.

World Wonders 4 Grammar Teacher's Book

The key to the student's book tasks is overprinted for easy reference. There are six photocopiable tests at the back of the teacher's book; one for every two units of *World Wonders 4 Grammar*. The key to the tests is also included.

Countable & Uncountable Nouns, Describing Quantities, Parts of Speech & Confusing Words

Countable & Uncountable Nouns

Countable nouns are nouns that we can count. They have both singular and plural forms. When the subject of a sentence is in the plural, then the verb must also be in the plural.
Jane's painting is beautiful.
Jane's paintings are beautiful.

Uncountable nouns are nouns that we cannot count. They don't have plural forms. When the subject of a sentence is an uncountable noun, then the verb must be in the singular.
Jenny's hair is very long.
Milk is good for you.

Remember! We don't use **a** or **an** with uncountable nouns.

1 Complete the table with these nouns.

apple   biscuit   cheese   cup   fork   homework
luggage   milk   money   pencil   toy   water

Countable	Uncountable
apple	cheese

Some & Any

We use **some** in affirmative sentences with plural countable nouns and uncountable nouns to say that something exists.
There are some letters on the table.
There's some milk in the glass.

We use **any** in negative sentences and in questions with plural countable nouns and uncountable nouns to say that something doesn't exist or to ask if something exists.
We don't have any free time today.
Are there any balls on the floor?

Remember! We can use the word **some** in questions when we ask for or offer something.
Can I have some water, please?
Can I get you some chips?

Describing quantities
Much & Many

We use **much** and **many** to describe quantity. We use **much** with uncountable nouns mainly in negative sentences and in questions.
There isn't *much* honey in the jar.
Have you got *much* work?

We use **many** with plural countable nouns mainly in negative sentences and in questions.
There aren't *many* children in the park.
Are there *many* flowers in the vase?

We use How much ...? and How many ...? when we ask about quantity. We use How much ...? for uncountable nouns and How many ...? for countable nouns.
How much water do you drink every day?
How many friends do you have?

A lot of, Lots of, A few & A little

We use **a lot of** or **lots of** with countable and uncountable nouns in affirmative and negative sentences and in questions.
I've got *lots of* books.
Paul hasn't got *a lot of* DVDs.
Have you visited *lots of* places?

We use **a few** with plural countable nouns in affirmative sentences and in questions to show that a small amount of something exists. It has a positive meaning.
Brian bought *a few* presents for his friends.
Do you want *a few* lollies?

We use **a little** with uncountable nouns in affirmative sentences and in questions to show that a small amount of something exists. It has a positive meaning.
There is *a little* jam left.
Can I have *a little* water, please?

Phrases describing quantity
We can make uncountable nouns countable by using the following phrases:
a piece of, a slice of, a cup of, a glass of, a carton of, a loaf of, a jar of, a bowl of, etc.
There was only *a slice of* cake left.

Remember!
We don't usually use *much* and *many* in affirmative sentences. We use *lots of* or *a lot of* instead.
My grandad has got *a lot of/lots of* money.
Jennifer owns *a lot of/lots of* hats.

2 Circle the correct words.

1 **How much** / How many money do you need?
2 Is there a few / **much** sugar in the jar?
3 We have **lots of** / many homework tonight.
4 I only sent **many** / a few Christmas cards.
5 There are a little / **some** apples in the basket.
6 I've got **a few** / a little money left so I can buy a newspaper.
7 Have you got much / **lots of** pencils?
8 Johnny doesn't have **many** / some computer games.
9 I don't have **any** / many time to go shopping.
10 How a few / **many** candles did Liz have on her birthday cake?

3 Complete the sentences. Use these phrases of quantity.

| a bottle of | a bowl of | a carton of | a cup of |
| a glass of | a jar of | a loaf of | a slice of |

1 Could you buy _____*a carton of*_____ juice, please?
2 Shall I make you _____ tea?
3 I have _____ cereal for breakfast.
4 Can I offer you _____ pizza?
5 Would you like _____ milk with your biscuits?
6 I always have _____ water in my bag.
7 My mum buys _____ honey every week!
8 George can eat _____ bread all by himself!

Parts of Speech
An **adjective** describes a noun.
A **noun** is a person, place or thing.
A **verb** expresses an action or state.
An **adverb** adds information to a verb or an adjective.
A **preposition** is used before a noun to show place, time, etc.
An **article** can be definite or indefinite.
A **modal verb** is a verb which is used with another verb.
A **pronoun** is used instead of a noun.

Lyn is a *beautiful* girl.
Cairo is very interesting.
Mick *kicked* the ball.
Jenny *quickly* got up.
There's somebody *at* the door.
Do you have *a* spare pen?
Cheetahs *can* run very fast.
It's John's bag. Give it to *him*.

4 Identify the parts of speech in bold.

1. Frank plays the guitar **beautifully**. — _adverb_
2. We **shouldn't** have made so much noise. — _____
3. My mum gave me a **beautiful** necklace. — _____
4. I'm sure I put my keys **on** the table. — _____
5. This isn't my hat. It must be **yours**. — _____
6. **Mel** is my best friend. — _____
7. Could I borrow **a** pencil, please? — _____
8. We **walked** around Ancient Olympia for hours. — _____

Confusing words
Confusing words are words that are very similar and therefore are often confused.

5 Choose the correct answers.

1. Please turn _____ the radio.
   a) off
   b) of

2. _____ waiting for Dad to pick them up.
   a) Their
   b) They're

3. Can you please be _____? I can't concentrate.
   a) quiet
   b) quite

4. _____ is this gorgeous puppy?
   a) Whose
   b) Who's

5. _____ a beautiful day! Let's go to the beach.
   a) Its
   b) It's

6. What do you think _____ rap music?
   a) off
   b) of

6 Write the contractions in bold in full.

1. **We'd** been waiting for an hour before the bus came. — _We had_
2. **There's** a spare seat here. — _____
3. Can you tell me **who's** making that noise? — _____
4. Oh no! **There's** been another attack! — _____
5. **It's** been great catching up. — _____
6. **We'd** go to the party if we had time. — _____

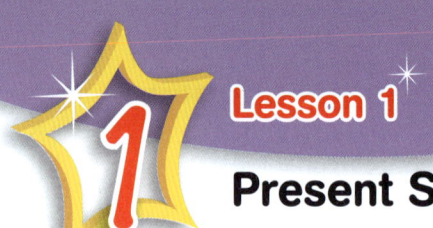

Lesson 1
Present Simple & Present Continuous

Present Simple

We use the **Present Simple** to talk about
- general truths.
  People in Brazil speak *Portuguese.*
- things that we do regularly.
  My cousin and I go *to the cinema every Saturday.*
- permanent situations.
  We live *in New York City.*
- timetabled and programmed events in the future.
  The auction begins *at five o'clock in the afternoon.*

Time expressions
The following **time expressions** go at the beginning or at the end of a sentence: **every day, at the weekend, in the morning, on Mondays, in January, on Friday evenings, twice a week,** etc.

Adverbs of Frequency
We use **adverbs of frequency** when we want to say how often something happens.

The following **adverbs of frequency** go before the main verb but after the verb **be**: **never, rarely, sometimes, often, usually, regularly, frequently, always.**
Natalie always hands in *her assignments on time.*
James is never *late for an appointment.*

We use **How often ...?** to ask about how often something happens.
How often do you go to the dentist?
Twice a year.

Affirmative	Negative	Question	Short answers	
I work	I don't work	Do I work ...?	Yes, I do.	No, I don't.
you work	you don't work	Do you work ...?	Yes, you do.	No, you don't.
he works	he doesn't work	Does he work ...?	Yes, he does.	No, he doesn't.
she works	she doesn't work	Does she work ...?	Yes, she does.	No, she doesn't.
it works	it doesn't work	Does it work ...?	Yes, it does.	No, it doesn't.
we work	we don't work	Do we work ...?	Yes, we do.	No, we don't.
you work	you don't work	Do you work ...?	Yes, you do.	No, you don't.
they work	they don't work	Do they work ...?	Yes, they do.	No, they don't.

1 Complete the sentences with the correct form of the Present Simple. Use the verbs in brackets.

1. Dad and I often _____make_____ noodles for lunch. (make)
2. My favourite football player _____ goals very often. (not score)
3. _____ you _____ your friends at the weekends? (meet)
4. Paula always _____ her hair before she goes out. (brush)
5. Timothy _____ his suitcase by himself. (not pack)
6. Karen always _____ to do the best she can. (try)
7. _____ the celebrity _____ in an apartment in Manhattan? (live)
8. The baby _____ all its milk. (not drink)

Present Continuous

We use the **Present Continuous** to talk about
- actions that are in progress at the time of speaking.
  The local department store is selling all designer clothes at 50% off today!
- actions that are in progress around the time of speaking.
  They are redecorating the Beverly Hills Hotel.
- actions that are temporary.
  Susan is working from home these days.
- future plans that we have arranged; they usually refer to the near future.
  We're visiting the National Gallery this Friday.
- annoying habits (with **always, constantly, forever**).
  Jodie is constantly forgetting her homework!
- changing situations.
  Your little brother is growing taller and taller every day.
- what is happening in a picture or photograph.
  The celebrity and her children are enjoying a walk in the park in this photo.

Time expressions
We often use the following **time expressions** with the **Present Continuous**: now, right now, at the moment, for the time being, today, these days, this morning/afternoon/week/year etc.
John is washing his bike at the moment.
Pamela is taking the bus to work these days.

Affirmative	Negative	Question	Short answers	
I'm staying	I'm not staying	Am I staying ...?	Yes, I am.	No, I'm not.
you're staying	you aren't staying	Are you staying ...?	Yes, you are.	No, you aren't.
he's staying	he isn't staying	Is he staying ...?	Yes, he is.	No, he isn't.
she's staying	she isn't staying	Is she staying ...?	Yes, she is.	No, she isn't.
it's staying	it isn't staying	Is it staying ...?	Yes, it is.	No, it isn't.
we're staying	we aren't staying	Are we staying ...?	Yes, we are.	No, we aren't.
you're staying	you aren't staying	Are you staying ...?	Yes, you are.	No, you aren't.
they're staying	they aren't staying	Are they staying ...?	Yes, they are.	No, they aren't.

---

2 Complete the sentences with the correct form of the Present Continuous. Use the words in brackets.

1. The weather _____is getting_____ warmer and warmer these days. (get)
2. Gregory _____ in a hotel because he prefers camping. (stay)
3. I can't come with you. I _____ for a maths test at the moment. (study)
4. _____ lunch with your colleagues tomorrow? (you / have)
5. My little brother _____ with my toys. (forever play)
6. _____ Grandma tomorrow? (they / visit)

3 Look at the pictures and complete the sentences with the correct form of the Present Continuous. Use these verbs.

> audition   enjoy   interview   listen   sign   watch

1 At the moment, Julia ___is auditioning___ for the reality show.

4 _____ you and your friends _____ yourselves?

2 This week, my favourite author _____ autographs for her new book.

5 The journalist _____ the gold medallist right now.

3 Mandy and her sister _____ a DVD this afternoon.

6 _____ Sandra _____ to music?

4 Circle the correct words.

1 Our train to Milan **departs** / is departing at eight o'clock tomorrow morning.
2 For the time being, the famous sculptor works / is working in San Francisco.
3 The local theatrical group performs / is performing every Friday evening in the park.
4 Dad is a journalist but he rarely interviews / is interviewing famous people.
5 In this photo my sister blows / is blowing out her candles.
6 Our school has / is having a book sale in the library next week.

5 Match.

1 Does your school frequently raise money for charity?   a No, she doesn't.
2 Are you travelling around Australia next month?   b Yes, I am.
3 Do newspapers always publish articles about the rich and famous. c Yes, it does.
4 Is the local football team playing on this pitch tomorrow?   d Yes, they are.
5 Are Freddie and Jane staying in their cousin's flat for the time being? e No, it isn't.
6 Does your mother work in a bank?   f No, they don't.

6 Choose the correct answers.

1 _____ with your family at the weekend?
   a) Do you often go away
   b) Are you often going away
   c) You often go away

2 It's so annoying. My neighbours _____ a lot of noise.
   a) are making always
   b) are always making
   c) always makes

3 At the moment, the actress _____ for her new role.
   a) rehearse
   b) rehearsing
   c) is rehearsing

4 _____ the best performer at the end of the competition?
   a) Does the judge choose
   b) Is the judge choosing
   c) Are the judges choosing

5 The party _____ until nine o'clock at night.
   a) doesn't start
   b) is starting
   c) starts

6 The price of petrol _____ more and more every day!
   a) increase
   b) is increasing
   c) increasing

7 Complete the telephone conversation with the Present Simple or the Present Continuous. Use the words in brackets.

Isabel: What's the matter, Dan?
Dan: It's my brother. He (1) __is constantly hiding__ (constantly hide) my DVDs.
Isabel: Oh dear. Listen, our favourite R & B group (2) _____ (go) on tour in a few months. Shall we get tickets?
Dan: I (3) _____ (not know). Our teacher (4) _____ (forever give) us lots of homework and the concert (5) _____ (not end) till late.
Isabel: True, but we (6) _____ (not get) the chance to see them often.
Dan: You're right. And they (7) _____ (record) their new album at the moment.
Isabel: (8) _____ then? (you / agree)
Dan: Yes!

Speaking

Look at the pictures and talk with your partner about how often you do these things. Use appropriate adverbs of frequency and time expressions.

I usually exercise every Saturday morning.

I always walk to school with my friends.

11

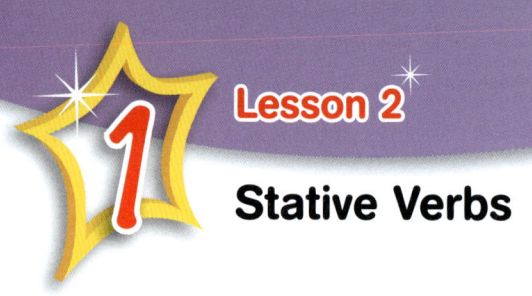

Lesson 2

Stative Verbs

Stative Verbs

Stative verbs describe states, not actions. We don't usually use **stative verbs** with the **Present Continuous**.
The most common **stative verbs** are:
verbs of senses:
feel, hear, see, smell, sound, taste
These noodles taste awful!

verbs of emotion:
dislike, hate, like, love, need, prefer, want
I prefer jeans to formal trousers.

verbs of understanding and opinion:
appear, believe, forget, hope, imagine, know, mean, realise, remember, seem, think, understand, wonder
Alice never remembers her facebook password.

verbs that show possession:
belong to, have, own, possess
This book belongs to John.

Some **stative verbs** can be used with the **Present Continuous**, but their meaning changes.
These verbs include:
appear, be, feel, have, look, see, think

The actor appears to be tired. (He looks tired.)
The jazz band is appearing at the local pub this weekend. (The band is performing.)

Penny went to bed because she has a bad headache. (Her head hurts.)
I'm having lunch at the moment. (I am eating lunch now.)

I feel happy about my success. (I am glad that I am successful.)
Sue is feeling the fabric to see if she likes it. (She is touching it.)

Jason looks really happy today. (He appears to be happy.)
What are you looking at? (What are you watching?)

Do you see the rainbow in the sky? (Are you able to see it?)
I'm seeing my old classmates this Saturday. (I have an appointment.)

Mrs Jones thinks that we should study every night. (She believes this.)
My parents are thinking of buying a new car. (They are considering this.)

1 Complete the sentences with the Present Simple or the Present Continuous. Use the verbs in brackets.

1. I __hear__ what you're saying but I don't agree. (hear)
2. _____ what I am saying? (you / understand)
3. Melinda _____ at the moment. She's looking for a new job. (not work)
4. This is such a nice T-shirt. I _____ it! (love)
5. The children are so happy. They _____ a wonderful time. (have)
6. It's not my dog. I _____ it. (not own)
7. We can either go to the park or to the cinema. What _____? (you / prefer)
8. I _____ about anything at the moment. (not think)

2 Write sentences with the Present Simple or the Present Continuous.

1. Fiona / dislike / romantic comedies / and / musicals
   Fiona dislikes romantic comedies and musicals.
2. Harriet / appear / in / a West End musical / next month
3. ? / you / remember / when / we met
4. ? / you / have / a meeting / with / the director / tomorrow morning
5. David Beckham / be / a very good football player.
6. my brother / constantly / forget / my birthday

3 Complete the sentences with the Present Simple or the Present Continuous. Use these verbs.

| have | look | not like | not think | see | think |

1. The musicians __are having__ dinner with the songwriter this evening.
2. This portrait _____ great in the living room.
3. Carrie _____ a doctor this afternoon about her broken arm.
4. I _____ the first track on this CD is too bad.
5. Yuk! I _____ this soup!
6. We _____ of going to the awards ceremony later this afternoon.

4 Complete the advertisement with the Present Simple or the Present Continuous. Use the verbs in brackets.

DREAMS DO COME TRUE!

(1) __Do__ you __believe__ (believe) in dreams coming true?
(2) _____ you _____ (want) to start a solo career?
We (3) _____ (look for) talented singers between 17 and 24 years old.
All you (4) _____ (need) is a good voice and the will to succeed.
If you (5) _____ (think) you're ready for stardom, we
(6) _____ (see) singers from all over the country next week.
Contact us on 0800 230970

5 Complete the dialogue with the Present Simple or the Present Continuous. Use these verbs.

love   not like   own   prefer   see   sound   want

Henrietta: George, (1) ____Do____ you ____want____ to do something different this summer?
George: Mm. That (2) _____ interesting!
Henrietta: There's a great Rock Festival in June.
George: Wow! I absolutely (3) _____ rock music! Yes, let's go!
Henrietta: Great. Let's book our flights.
George: Flights? Oh, maybe not. I (4) _____ flying. It's scary.
Henrietta: I (5) _____ what you mean.
George: I (6) _____ going to a festival in England.
Henrietta: Well, there's a Rock Fest in Cambridge. Let me see.
George: Great! My family (7) _____ a house in Cambridge. We can stay there!

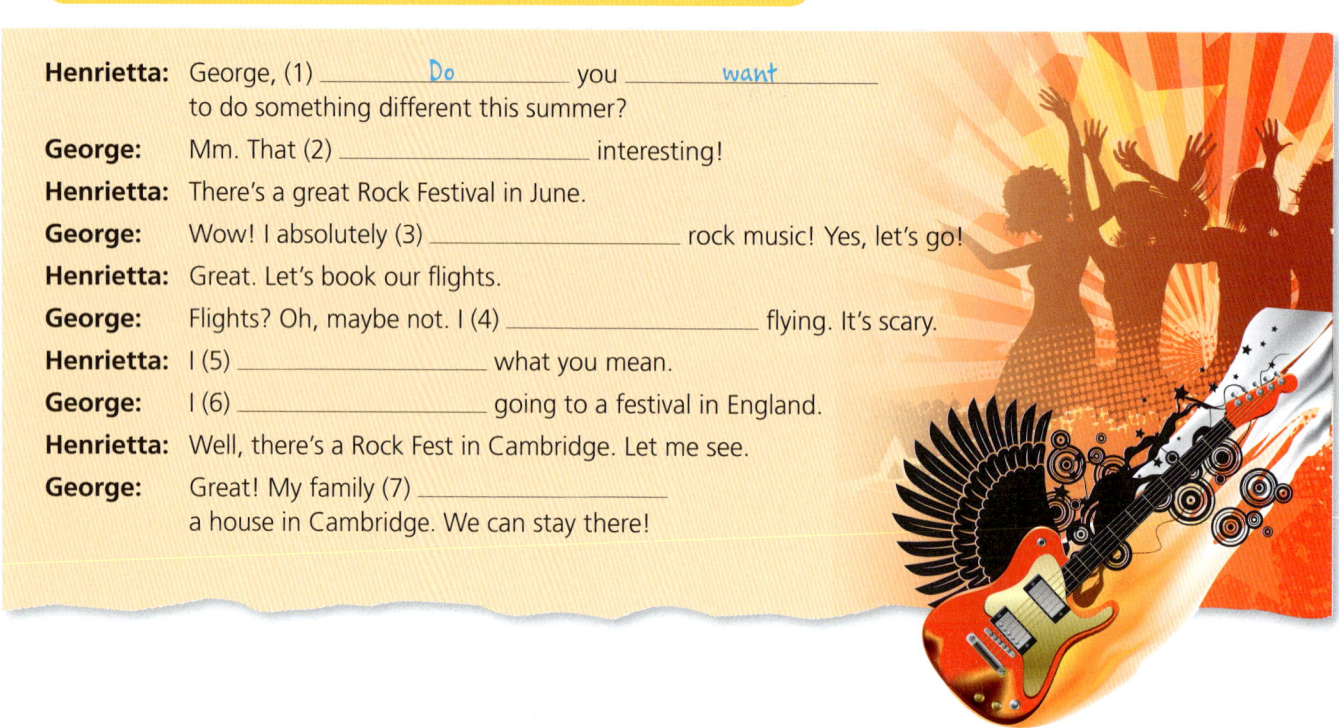

Speaking

Talk to your partner about what you would say in these situations. Use stative verbs.

- You are talking to a new friend about what you like and don't like.
- You tried a new dish and you are describing it to your mum.
- Your teacher has asked the class to tell him your opinions about recycling.

I really like hip hop music.

Actually, I prefer classical music.

Lesson 3

Direct & Indirect Objects

Direct & Indirect Objects

Some sentences have two objects, a direct object and an indirect object. We can usually identify the **direct object** by asking **what**. If the direct object is a person, we can identify it by asking **who**.

My parents bought me a new computer.
Q: **What** did my parents buy?
A: a **new computer** (direct object)

My dad took me to the party.
Q: **Who** did your dad take to the party?
A: **me** (direct object)

We can identify the **indirect object** by asking the questions **for/to whom** or **for/to what**.

My parents bought me a new computer.
Q: **For whom** did they buy it?
A: **me** (indirect object)

My dad took me to the party.
Q: **To what** did your dad take you?
A: **the party** (indirect object)

The **indirect object** comes before the **direct object** in a sentence.
Jane gave Mark a beautiful T-shirt.
Mum made me a fantastic birthday cake.

We can also write these sentences using a prepositional phrase with **to** or **for**.
Jane gave a beautiful T-shirt to Mark.
Mum made a fantastic birthday cake for me.

However, sentences which use verbs such as **ask** and **cost**, cannot be rewritten using a prepositional phrase.
I asked my mother a question.
The painting cost Jane a lot of money.

1 **Underline the direct objects and circle the indirect objects.**

1 The director offered (me) the part.
2 The magician showed us a white rabbit.
3 The fans sent the actress emails.
4 Dad bought Mum some flowers.
5 I told my teacher a little white lie.
6 The tourist lent me his camera.

2 **Rewrite the sentences using a prepositional phrase with to or for.**

1 Dad bought us a huge carton of popcorn.
   Dad bought a huge carton of popcorn for us.
2 Our school always gives poverty-stricken children money.

3 Serena told her parents a hilarious joke.

4 I've already given you three of my new CDs!

5 We showed the tourists Mount Lycabettus.

6 Did you bring me the theatre tickets?

3 **Find the mistakes and write the sentences correctly.**

1 David is buying a diamond ring her.
   David is buying a diamond ring for her/her a diamond ring.
2 Daddy, Daddy! Buy for me some candy!

3 The bank manager is going to send a reply me.

4 Will showed us to the stars through his telescope.

5 My penfriend sends to me a letter every month.

6 We made a beautiful birthday card to our teacher.

4 Put the words in the correct order to write sentences.

1 is / ball / me / throwing / to / he / the
   He is throwing the ball to me.

2 tonight / you / for / am / I / paying

3 a difficult question / asked / Mr Ledson / me

4 are / they / us / dinner / cooking

5 homework / gives / your / a lot of / teacher / you

6 on / you / spend / much / too / DVDs / money

7 they / car / him / are / their / showing

8 didn't cost / my / me / a lot of money / new laptop

Speaking

Look at the cards with a partner and use the prompts to talk about these situations.

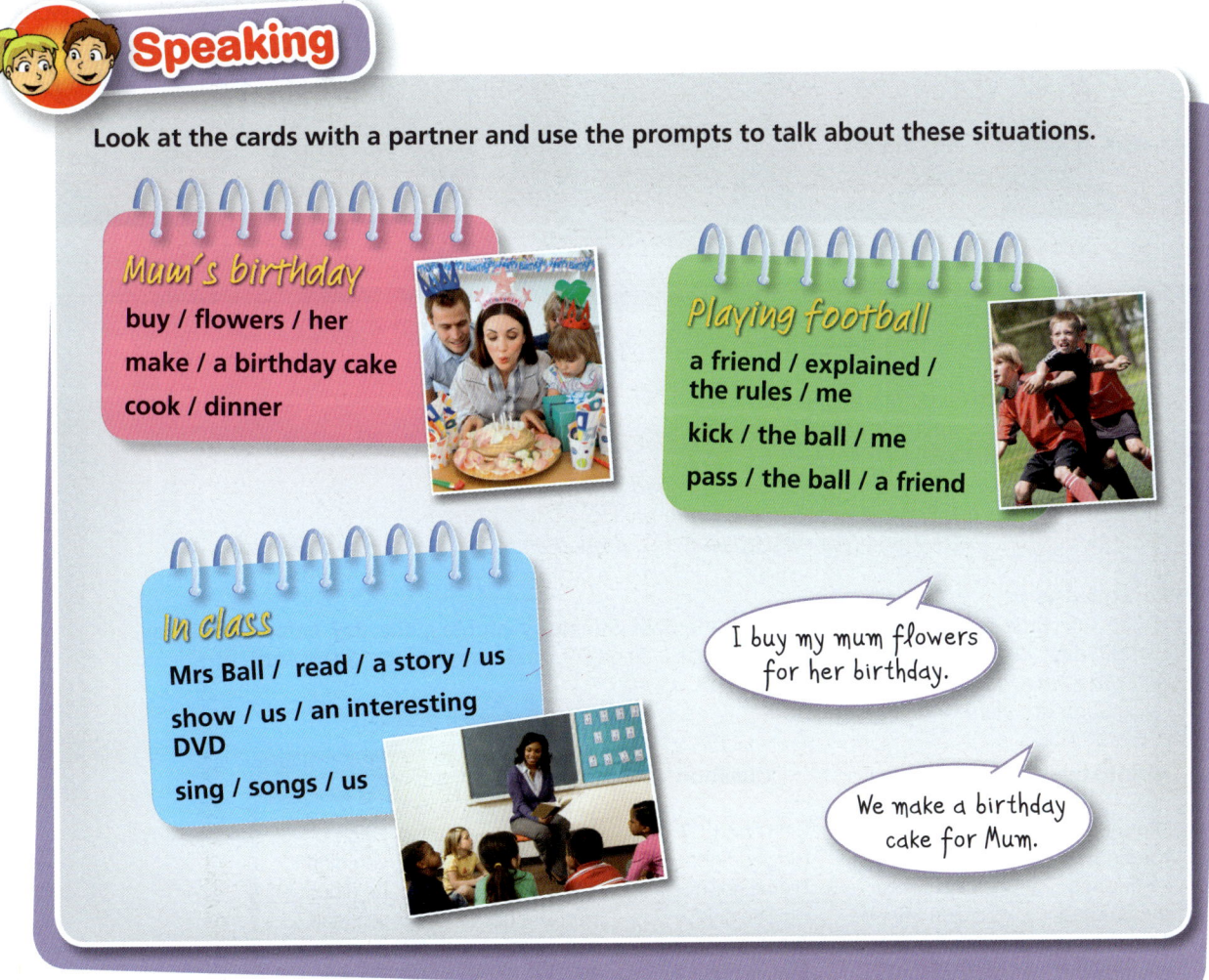

Mum's birthday
buy / flowers / her
make / a birthday cake
cook / dinner

Playing football
a friend / explained / the rules / me
kick / the ball / me
pass / the ball / a friend

In class
Mrs Ball / read / a story / us
show / us / an interesting DVD
sing / songs / us

I buy my mum flowers for her birthday.

We make a birthday cake for Mum.

Lesson 1
Past Simple & Past Continuous

Past Simple

We use the **Past Simple** to talk about
- actions that started and finished in the past.
  Peter won the 100-metre race yesterday.
- past habits.
  I watched cartoons every Saturday morning when I was younger.
- actions that happened one after the other in the past.
  Andrew climbed to the top of the mountain, looked around and took a picture of the view.

Time expressions
The following **time expressions** are used with the **Past Simple**: yesterday, the day before yesterday, the other day, last week, a week ago, in January, in 2009, last summer, on 21st April, etc.
I went on an excursion the day before yesterday.
My grandparents went on a cruise last week.

Affirmative	Negative	Question	Short answers	
I finished	I didn't finish	Did I finish ...?	Yes, I did.	No, I didn't.
you finished	you didn't finish	Did you finish ...?	Yes, you did.	No, you didn't.
he finished	he didn't finish	Did he finish ...?	Yes, he did.	No, he didn't.
she finished	she didn't finish	Did she finish ...?	Yes, she did.	No, she didn't.
it finished	it didn't finish	Did it finish ...?	Yes, it did.	No, it didn't.
we finished	we didn't finish	Did we finish ...?	Yes, we did.	No, we didn't.
you finished	you didn't finish	Did you finish ...?	Yes, you did.	No, you didn't.
they finished	they didn't finish	Did they finish ...?	Yes, they did.	No, they didn't.

See the Irregular verbs list on page 159.

1 **Complete the sentences with the Past Simple. Use the verbs in brackets.**

1. When Nicola was ten years old, she _____painted_____ her first portrait. (paint)
2. Last year, Thomas _____ for two months in Cambridge at Summer School. (study)
3. Henry VI _____ King of England in 1422. (become)
4. Two years ago, we _____ around Europe. (drive)
5. My little brother _____ all his toy dinosaurs in the park this morning. (lose)
6. We _____ our suitcases, _____ the car and _____ on our journey. (pack, get in, set off)

Past Continuous
We use the **Past Continuous** to
- talk about an action that was in progress at a specific time in the past.
  At three o'clock yesterday afternoon, we were walking through Hyde Park.
- talk about two or more actions that were in progress at the same time in the past. We use **and** or **while** to connect the actions.
  I was writing an email and Jessie was speaking to her cousin on skype.
  Nancy was watching a DVD while Peter was making sandwiches.
- to describe the scene of a story.
  The sun was shining, the children were playing in the garden and their parents were chatting.
- talk about an action that was in progress in the past that was interrupted by another action.
  We were dancing when the music stopped.

Time expressions
We often use the following **time expressions** with the **Past Continuous**: all morning, all day yesterday, at six o'clock, last year, this morning, this time last week, from nine to five, etc.
My parents were painting my bedroom all day yesterday.
I was playing tennis this morning.

Affirmative	Negative	Question	Short answers	
I was sleeping	I wasn't sleeping	Was I sleeping ...?	Yes, I was.	No, I wasn't.
you were sleeping	you weren't sleeping	Were you sleeping ...?	Yes, you were.	No, you weren't.
he was sleeping	he wasn't sleeping	Was he sleeping ...?	Yes, he was.	No, he wasn't.
she was sleeping	she wasn't sleeping	Was she sleeping ...?	Yes, she was.	No, she wasn't.
it was sleeping	it wasn't sleeping	Was it sleeping ...?	Yes, it was.	No, it wasn't.
we were sleeping	we weren't sleeping	Were we sleeping ...?	Yes, we were.	No, we weren't.
you were sleeping	you weren't sleeping	Were you sleeping ...?	Yes, you were.	No, you weren't.
they were sleeping	they weren't sleeping	Were they sleeping ...?	Yes, they were.	No, they weren't.

---

2 **Complete the sentences with the Past Continuous. Use these verbs.**

| drive | enjoye | have | not play | pack | read | not sail | shine | sing | walk |

1. I _____was walking_____ home when it started to rain.
2. _____ you _____ your suitcases all last night?
3. At eight o'clock last night, the twins _____ an adventure film.
4. Last summer, we _____ around the Greek islands.
5. My little brother _____ with his dinosaurs all morning.
6. During the trip, Nancy _____ the car and I _____ the map.
7. It was a glorious day! The birds _____ and the sun _____ .
8. _____ David _____ a meeting when you called him this morning?

Past Simple & Past Continuous

We use the **Past Simple** and the **Past Continuous** in the same sentence when
- an action that was in progress in the past was interrupted by another action.
  We were watching a DVD when our cousins arrived.
- we tell a story in the past.
  I was walking down the street when I bumped into Angela.

3 Complete Tracey's diary entry with the Past Simple or the Past Continuous. Use the verbs in brackets.

Yesterday I had a great day! I woke up, got dressed and (1) **left** (leave) home at half past eight. While I (2) _____ (walk) to school, I met my friend Jenny. It was the day of the school trip to the archaeological museum and we (3) _____ (be) very excited.

When we (4) _____ (get) to school, the bus was leaving so we ran to catch it! The journey to the museum was fun, too. While the bus driver (5) _____ (drive), we were listening to music and singing.

At the museum, we (6) _____ (see) beautiful sculptures and vases. While we (7) _____ (admire) the exhibits, Jenny shouted 'Look!' and she ran towards the Egyptian art collection.

I (8) _____ (try) to find Jenny when I saw our favourite singer. Jenny was standing next to him. She was giving him a pen and he was smiling at her! Jenny was so happy because he gave her his autograph.

As, When & While

We usually use **as**, **when** and **while** to connect two actions.

We use **as/when** before the **Past Simple**
- to refer to two short actions which happened at the same time.
  As I opened my eyes, I saw a bright light.

We use **when** before the **Past Simple** for
- a short action that interrupted a long action.
  They were having dinner when the phone rang.
- a short action that happened immediately after another short action.
  I caught the ball when Joe threw it.

We also use **when** to talk about
- a person's age when something happened.
  When Vicky was five, she went to school.
- a period of a person's life when something happened.
  When Ricky was a teenager, he won a skateboarding competition.

We usually use **while** before the **Past Continuous** to talk about
- two long actions that were happening at the same time.
  Jake was watching a DVD while his sister was tidying her room.

We usually use **as/while** before the **Past Continuous** to talk about
- a long action that was happening when a short action interrupted it.
  As/While Julie was walking home, it started to rain.

4 Complete the sentences with as, when or while.

1. It was pouring with rain _____when_____ the sun came out.
2. _____ Frank put down the phone, the electricity went off.
3. Janet fell off her bike _____ she was cycling to work.
4. _____ I was locking the front door, I dropped my keys.
5. We were watching the World Cup on TV _____ Brazil scored a goal.
6. _____ you were sleeping, your little sister was playing games on your PSP.
7. I watched _____ the firemen tried to put out the fire.
8. I was looking through the trunk _____ I came across Grandma's old possessions.

5 Write sentences with the Past Simple or the Past Continuous.

1. we / admire / the sculptures / when / the lights go / out
   We were admiring the sculptures when the lights went out.
2. as / I jog / along the beach / I catch / a glimpse of / a famous celebrity
   _____
3. ? / Natalie / dress / for the party / when / the taxi / arrive
   _____
4. John / take / photos / of the Eiffel Tower / while / Judy / choose / postcards
   _____
5. ? / you / surf / the Net / when / you / drop / your laptop
   _____
6. Mr and Mrs Long / sleep / when / they / hear / a loud noise
   _____
7. as / the children / swim / the / see / a shark
   _____
8. the football star / talk / to his fans / while / he / sign / autographs
   _____

6 Complete the text with the Past Simple or the Past Continuous. Use the verbs in brackets.

The *Titanic* (1) _____was_____ (be) the largest passenger ship in the world at the time of its construction. It (2) _____ (begin) its voyage on 10th April 1912, but it never (3) _____ (reach) its destination.

What (4) _____ (happen) on the night of the disaster? Just before midnight, as the ship (5) _____ (sail), two members of the crew (6) _____ (see) a huge iceberg directly in front of the ship. They (7) _____ (try) to change the ship's course, but the iceberg was too close. The *Titanic* (8) _____ (hit) the iceberg and the side of the ship was badly damaged. This caused the ship to start flooding.

While the captain tried to get help, the crew (9) _____ (help) passengers into the lifeboats. Unfortunately the *Titanic* (10) _____ (not carry) enough lifeboats for everyone on board, so many people died.

 **Speaking**

Look at Josh and Kelly's diary with your partner. Ask and answer questions about what Josh and Kelly did on Saturday.

	JOSH	KELLY
8 am	woke up	was asleep
12 pm	watched documentary about Peru	went to shops to look for costume for party
2 pm	had lunch with Dad	visited Natural History Museum
4 pm	surfed Net for information about pyramids	rang Josh
8 pm	read comics	got ready for party
12 am	was asleep	came back from party

What time did Josh wake up?

He woke up at eight o'clock.

What was Kelly doing at eight o'clock in the morning?

She was sleeping.

Lesson 2

Used to & Would

Used to

We use **used to** talk about
- actions that we often did in the past but we no longer do.
  I used to enjoy playing board games.
- situations that existed in the past but don't exist now.
  My family and I used to live in a cottage.

Used to is followed by the infinitive of the main verb without **to** (bare infinitive).
Rebecca used to ride her bike to school.

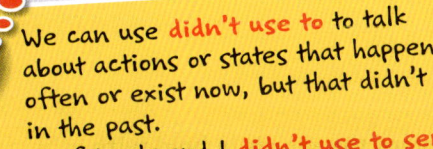

Remember!
We can use **didn't use to** to talk about actions or states that happen often or exist now, but that didn't in the past.
My friends and I didn't use to send text messages. (but we do now)

Affirmative	Negative	Question	Short answers	
I used to enjoy	I didn't use to enjoy	Did I use to enjoy ...?	Yes, I did.	No, I didn't.
you used to enjoy	you didn't use to enjoy	Did you use to enjoy ...?	Yes, you did.	No, you didn't.
he used to enjoy	he didn't use to enjoy	Did he use to enjoy ...?	Yes, he did.	No, he didn't.
she used to enjoy	she didn't use to enjoy	Did she use to enjoy ...?	Yes, she did.	No, she didn't.
it used to enjoy	it didn't use to enjoy	Did it use to enjoy ...?	Yes, it did.	No, it didn't.
we used to enjoy	we didn't use to enjoy	Did we use to enjoy ...?	Yes, we did.	No, we didn't.
you used to enjoy	you didn't use to enjoy	Did you use to enjoy ...?	Yes, you did.	No, you didn't.
they used to enjoy	they didn't use to enjoy	Did they use to enjoy ...?	Yes, they did.	No, they didn't.

1 Complete the sentences with the correct form of **used to**. Use the verbs in brackets.

1. In Spain, bullfighting _____used to be_____ a sport for the aristocracy. (be)
2. The Berlin Wall _____ East and West Germany. (separate)
3. We _____ Internet at home so I couldn't chat with my friends. (have)
4. _____ you _____ to school by yourself? (walk)
5. Jeremy _____ basketball, but now he does. (play)
6. _____ Katy and Isabel _____ a room at university? (share)

Would

We use **would** to talk about actions that we often did in the past but we no longer do.
We would always go to school by bus.

We can't use **would** to talk about states in the past and we don't usually use the negative form (wouldn't).

Affirmative	Negative	Question	Short answers	
I would visit	I wouldn't visit	Would I visit …?	Yes, I would.	No, I wouldn't.
you would visit	you wouldn't visit	Would you visit …?	Yes, you would.	No, you wouldn't.
he would visit	he wouldn't visit	Would he visit …?	Yes, he would.	No, he wouldn't.
she would visit	she wouldn't visit	Would she visit …?	Yes, she would.	No, she wouldn't.
it would visit	it wouldn't visit	Would it visit …?	Yes, it would.	No, it wouldn't.
we would visit	we wouldn't visit	Would we visit …?	Yes, we would.	No, we wouldn't.
you would visit	you wouldn't visit	Would you visit …?	Yes, you would.	No, you wouldn't.
they would visit	they wouldn't visit	Would they visit …?	Yes, they would.	No, they wouldn't.

2 Complete the sentences with the correct form of **would**. Use these verbs.

cry   invite   read   take   tell   win

1 Grandad ____would____ always ____tell____ us stories about the Second World War.
2 _____ your classmates _____ you to parties?
3 I saw many wonderful sights when I was young because my parents _____ me on many holidays.
4 My little sister _____ cry all the time when she was a baby.
5 Ryan _____ never _____ science fiction books when he was younger.
6 _____ Alexander the Great always _____ his battles?

3 Replace the words in bold with **would** where possible.

1 **Did** I **use to** like noodles when I was younger?   ____–____
2 Joseph **used to** guess the ending of every film we saw.   _____
3 The film star **didn't use to** be so stunning.   _____
4 Our football team **used to** often win the championship.   _____
5 **Did** you **use to** read gossip magazines when you were a teenager?   _____
6 A decade ago, there **didn't use to** be so many blocks of flats in my neighbourhood.   _____

4 Circle the correct words.

1 Wendy (used to) / would live in Madrid.
2 My friends and I didn't used / would play in the park after school.
3 My mum would / used to have blonde hair.
4 I didn't use to / would like thrillers but I do now.
5 My brother would / use to borrow our dad's car.
6 Did you use to / Would you believe in Father Christmas?

5 Choose the correct answers.

When I was still at school, my family and I (1) _____ to spend the weekends in the city. We (2) _____ a house in the countryside near a beautiful lake, and we went there every Friday evening.

On Saturdays, Mum and I (3) _____ to go to the village, we (4) _____ stay home. Dad and Ben, my brother, (5) _____ to go to the local football matches and Ben (6) _____ home a signed copy of his ticket. On Sundays we sometimes went sailing and out for lunch altogether.

What (7) _____ most? Sailing, but we (8) _____ go sailing if the weather was good.

1	a	didn't use	b	used to	c	would
2	a	used to own	b	would own	c	use to own
3	a	not used to	b	wouldn't	c	didn't use
4	a	used just to	b	would just	c	used just
5	a	would	b	used	c	use
6	a	would often bring	b	would bring often	c	used often bring
7	a	would like	b	we would like	c	did we use to like
8	a	used only	b	would only	c	did use only

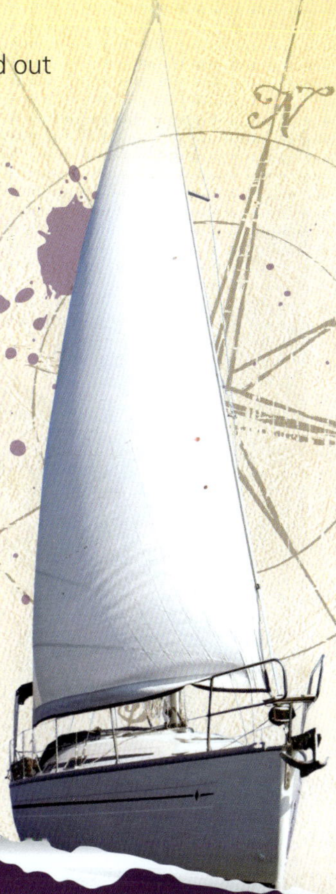

(1) a is circled.

Speaking

Talk with you partner about how life used to be and what people would do fifty years ago. Use would, used to and these suggestions to help you.

- people were more relaxed
- cities were less polluted
- children did less homework
- more greenery
- not many supermarkets
- have Internet
- write letters

Children used to have more free time.

Most people would walk more.

Lesson 3

Used to, Get used to & Be used to

Used to

We use **used to + bare infinitive** to talk about actions that happened often in the past or states that existed in the past but don't now.
Sandy *used to help* me with my Latin homework.
My teacher *used to live* in Japan.

Remember! In the negative and question form we use **use to** and not **used to**.

1 Complete the sentences with the correct form of **used to** and the verbs in brackets.

1 Many years ago, explorers _____used to travel_____ by ship. (travel)
2 _____ you _____ milk before you went to bed? (drink)
3 At the beginning of the 20th century, many Greeks _____ in Alexandria. (live)
4 _____ your parents _____ by coach or plane? (travel)
5 My mother _____ soap operas but now she does. (watch)
6 _____ Sol Campbell _____ for Tottenham Hotspur? (play)

Get used to

We use **get used to** + **-ing** or a noun to talk about actions or states that are becoming familiar to us.

We can use **get used to** with all tenses and with modal verbs.
I'm getting used to wearing a school uniform.
We *should get used to eating* more healthily.

Affirmative	Negative	Question	Short answers	
I get used to tying	I don't get used to tying	Do I get used to tying ...?	Yes, I do.	No, I don't.
you get used to tying	you don't get used to tying	Do you get used to tying ...?	Yes, you do.	No, you don't.
he gets used to tying	he doesn't get used to tying	Does he get used to tying ...?	Yes, he does.	No, he doesn't.
she gets used to tying	she doesn't get used to tying	Does she get used to tying ...?	Yes, she does.	No, she doesn't.
it gets used to tying	it doesn't get used to tying	Does it get used to tying ...?	Yes, it does.	No, it doesn't.
we get used to tying	we don't get used to tying	Do we get used to tying ...?	Yes, we do.	No, we don't.
you get used to tying	you don't get used to tying	Do you get used to tying ...?	Yes, you do.	No, you don't.
they get used to tying	they don't get used to tying	Do they get used to tying ...?	Yes, they do.	No, they don't.

2 Complete the sentences using the correct form of **get used to** and these verbs.

> drive   live   speak   use   wake up   work

1. After complaining for a year, Dad finally _got used to working_ in the city centre.
2. Evan must _____ at seven o'clock in the morning.
3. Hannah _____ a computer yet.
4. It's difficult to _____ in a foreign country.
5. I tried very hard but I couldn't _____ on the left-hand side of the road.
6. Mark _____ in English now.

3 Write questions using the correct form of **get used to**.

1. _Are you getting used to your new routine?_
   Yes, I'm getting used to my new routine.
2. _____
   No, we won't get used to living in a remote area.
3. _____
   Yes, the new ruler will get used to being in power.
4. _____
   No, Tamara and Alex haven't got used to their new drama teacher.
5. _____
   Yes, you should get used to the residents in this small community.
6. _____
   No, Thomas isn't getting used to working in the museum.

Be used to

We use **be used to** + **-ing** or a noun to talk about actions or states that are no longer unusual.

We can use **be used to** with all tenses apart from the continuous tenses and modal verbs.
Helena is used to cycling to work.
I am used to having cereal for breakfast.

Affirmative	Negative	Question	Short answers	
I'm used to writing	I'm not used to writing	Am I used to writing …?	Yes, I am.	No, I'm not.
you're used to writing	you aren't used to writing	Are you used to writing …?	Yes, you are.	No, you aren't.
he's used to writing	he isn't used to writing	Is he used to writing …?	Yes, he is.	No, he isn't.
she's used to writing	she isn't used to writing	Is she used to writing …?	Yes, she is.	No, she isn't.
it's used to writing	it isn't used to writing	Is it used to writing …?	Yes, it is.	No, it isn't.
we're used to writing	we aren't used to writing	Are we used to writing …?	Yes, we are.	No, we aren't.
you're used to writing	you aren't used to writing	Are you used to writing …?	Yes, you are.	No, you aren't.
they're used to writing	they aren't used to writing	Are they used to writing …?	Yes, they are.	No, they aren't.

4 Look at the situations and write sentences with the correct form of **be used to**.

1 Veronica is trying to send an email but she is having difficulty.
   Veronica isn't used to sending emails.

2 Our mum always cooks healthy food so we never eat anything else.
   _____

3 When we moved to the country, Dad started cycling to work. It was difficult for him.
   _____

4 These days, most teachers can use interactive whiteboards.
   _____

5 When we lived in England it rained a lot but it didn't bother us.
   _____

6 I don't go out for lunch during the week.
   _____

5 Complete the questions using the correct form of **be used to** and then write short answers.

1 ? / Lucy / knit
Is Lucy used to knitting?
No, she isn't.

4 ? / Billy and Neil / write / text messages
_____

2 ? / Jason / water-skiing
_____

5 ? / Mr Stevens / fly
_____

3 ? / your grandmother / use / a computer
_____

6 ? / the girls / wear / a school uniform
_____

6 Match.

1. Don't be shy! You should get used
2. When I was at boarding school in Kent, I
3. Did Isabella use
4. Now that I'm on a diet,
5. Nicky's mum worked long hours so Nicky was used to
6. Before she became rich and famous, Gina didn't

a. to go to summer school in England?
b. to speaking in front of an audience.
c. use to earn a lot of money.
d. used to wear a school uniform.
e. I'm getting used to eating more fruit and vegetables.
f. cooking for herself.

7 Complete the text with the correct form of **used to**, **get used to**, **be used to** and the verbs in brackets.

My classmates and I never (1) _____used to like_____ (like) history in the past.
We (2) _____ (think) it was boring, as we could never
(3) _____ (learn) dates of important battles and historical events.
Then, six months ago, Mrs Hatton arrived at our school and we slowly
(4) _____ (study) in a different way. She encouraged us to
use small cards and to write dates and a summary of the battle or event on each card.
At the time, we (5) _____ (not make) an effort,
but we all decided to give it a try. Of course, it worked! Now,
we (6) _____ (memorise) the
information on our cards and the exams are so much easier!

Speaking

Imagine that have moved to a foreign country. Talk with your partner about what you have to get used to now and about what you used to do before. Use these suggestions to help you.

- new school
- learn a foreign language
- different way of life
- speak my language at school
- feel comfortable in my neighbourhood
- have a lot of friends

I am getting used to my new teachers.

I used to know a lot of people.

Units 1 & 2

1 Complete Helen's profile. Use the Present Simple or the Present Continuous. Use these verbs.

be   collect   have   live   meet   play   speak   travel   work

Who's new in the Music World?

Helen Colet (1) ___is___ from London, England and right now, she (2) _____ in Milan. She (3) _____ English and Italian and for the time being, she (4) _____ as a music journalist. Helen (5) _____ vintage guitars and she (6) _____ basketball every Friday evening. This weekend, she (7) _____ lunch with a famous songwriter. She (8) _____ him in Rome. This summer Helen (9) _____ to Thailand.

2 Complete the dialogue with the Present Simple or the Present Continuous. Use the verbs in brackets.

Stephanie: (1) ___Do you remember___ (you / remember) Delia from school?
Gregory: Delia Hamilton?
Stephanie: That's right. I (2) _____ (see) her this week.
(3) _____ (you / want) to come?
Gregory: Well I (4) _____ (not have) very much free time, but …
Stephanie: Anyhow, she (5) _____ (have) a dinner party on Friday night. Can you come?
Gregory: Of course. I really (6) _____ (like) dinner parties. Delia Hamilton! I can't wait to see her!
Stephanie: She still (7) _____ (look) great. By the way, she (8) _____ (think) of having the party where her parents lived in the country.
Gregory: (9) _____ (the house / belong) to her now?
Stephanie: Yes, it does.
Gregory: A dinner party in the countryside. That (10) _____ (seem) like a great idea!
Stephanie: Yes, it does.

3 Complete the sentences with the Past Simple or the Past Continuous. Use the verbs in brackets.

1 India ___became___ independent on 15th August, 1947. (become)
2 I _____ the review, _____ the tickets and _____ the film. (read, buy, see)
3 As the athlete _____ the finish line, he collapsed. (cross)
4 In 2005, Fernando Alonso _____ his first Formula 1 title. (win)
5 While Laurie _____ the thriller, he _____ a loud noise. (watch, hear)
6 Isabel _____ the dog while her sister _____ . (walk, jog)
7 The guitarist _____ his story to the journalist. (sell)
8 The dog _____ a huge hole in the garden when Dad _____ him! (dig, watch)
9 Our teacher _____ us a leaflet about Drummond Castle and _____ us to read it quietly. (give, ask)
10 Lynn _____ photos of the Pyramids when she suddenly _____ ill. (take, feel)

4 Complete the magazine article with the Past Simple or the Past Continuous. Use the verbs in brackets.

Jennifer Aniston in brief

Jennifer Aniston (1) ____grew up____ (grow up) in New York and she (2) _____ (start) her acting career at the age of eleven when she (3) _____ (join) her school's drama club. While she (4) _____ (study) at school, she (5) _____ (become) interested in many forms of art. She (6) _____ (be) a talented painter but acting also (7) _____ (appeal) to her. After graduating, acting became her primary focus.

After a few minor roles, Aniston (8) _____ (consider) giving up acting, but her plans (9) _____ (change) in 1994 when a part in the series *Friends* (10) _____ (come) along. *Friends* became a worldwide success and so did she!

5 Circle the correct words.

1. You would use / **Did you use to use** a dictionary for your French homework?
2. We would listen / didn't use listen to classical music when we were younger.
3. Did the secretary use / Would the secretary arrive at the office on time?
4. He would be / used to be a popular fashion designer.
5. I would / didn't use to like olives on my pizza.
6. Felicity would / didn't use dream of fame and fortune.

6 Rewrite the second sentences using the correct form of **used to** or **get used to** so the meaning is similar to the first sentences.

1. The singer is starting to feel more comfortable about performing live.
   The singer ____is getting used____ to performing live.
2. I didn't enter competitions when I was young, but now I do.
   I _____ competitions.
3. Sooner or later, our new neighbourhood won't feel so unusual.
   Sooner or later, we will _____ our new neighbourhood.
4. Paying a lot of money for clothes is something new for us.
   We _____ a lot of money for clothes.
5. Does Sandra feel odd working such long hours?
   Is Sandra _____ such long hours?
6. I soon learnt to speak French when I lived in Paris.
   I _____ speaking French when I lived in Paris.

7 The words in bold are wrong. Write the correct words.

1. Jane **being** used to life as a celebrity. ____is____
2. Eric **would** like science, but now he hates it! _____
3. These days, I am used to **be** interviewed by the press. _____
4. In ancient times, the Greek gods used to **living** on Mount Olympus. _____
5. Are you finally **being** used to catching the underground to Trafalgar Square? _____
6. The Olympic Games used to **taking** place in Olympia. _____

Review 1
Units 1 & 2

Writing Project

1 Look at this writing project about Rome. Circle the correct words.

Rome (1) is boasting / **boasts** a history of over 2,500 years. People (2) believe / are believing that Romulus founded Rome on 21st April, 753 BC and there is proof that people (3) are used to living / used to live there 14,000 years ago. Rome was a monarchy, a republic and then an empire, which (4) was used to / used to dominate most of Europe. The Roman Emperors (5) were used to winning / are getting used to winning their battles. However, the Muslim Arabs tried many times to conquer Rome, and eventually the Romans (6) lost / would lose.

Rome (7) was always being / was always an important city throughout the Middle Ages and the Renaissance. In 1871, it (8) was becoming / became capital of modern Italy.

Rome is full of monuments, parks and fountains. Sites (9) are including / include the Vatican City, the Trevi fountain and the magnificent Colosseum. Here, in ancient times, citizens (10) are used to watching / would watch gladiators fighting. Now, the Colosseum (11) receives / is receiving approximately 4 million tourists per year.

Rome certainly (12) is / is being the Eternal City.

2 Now it's your turn to do a project about a famous historical city. Find or draw a picture of this city and write about it.

Lesson 1

Present Perfect Simple, Present Perfect Continuous & Present Perfect Simple vs Present Perfect Continuous

Present Perfect Simple

We use the **Present Perfect Simple** to talk about something that
- started in the past but hasn't finished.
  We**'ve been** members of this club for six years.
- has just finished.
  Sam **has just finished** the poster.
- happened in the past but we don't know or we don't say exactly when.
  Kelly **has won** three silver medals.
- happened in the past but that affects the present.
  I**'ve broken** my arm so I can't come skiing.

See the list of past participles on page 159.

Remember!
We use **have been** when someone went somewhere and has returned.
My parents and I **have been** to Disneyland.
We use **have gone** when someone went somewhere and hasn't returned yet.
Natalie isn't at school. She**'s gone** home.

Time expressions

We use the following **time expressions** with the **Present Perfect Simple**: already, ever, for, just, never, since, still, yet.
We have known each other **since** 2004.
Philip has **already** started the project.

Affirmative	Negative	Question	Short answers	
I've become	I haven't become	Have I become ...?	Yes, I have.	No, I haven't.
you've become	you haven't become	Have you become ...?	Yes, you have.	No, you haven't.
he's become	he hasn't become	Has he become ...?	Yes, he has.	No, he hasn't.
she's become	she hasn't become	Has she become ...?	Yes, she has.	No, she hasn't.
it's become	it hasn't become	Has it become ...?	Yes, it has.	No, it hasn't.
we've become	we haven't become	Have we become ...?	Yes, we have.	No, we haven't.
you've become	you haven't become	Have you become ...?	Yes, you have.	No, you haven't.
they've become	they haven't become	Have they become ...?	Yes, they have.	No, they haven't.

1 Complete the sentences with the Present Perfect Simple. Use the verbs in brackets.

1 My classmates and I _have taken part_ in the kayaking race three times. (take part)
2 We _____ at this restaurant before. (not eat)
3 The weatherman _____ just _____ rain for tomorrow morning. (forecast)
4 David _____ the darts competition twice this year. (win)
5 _____ to a concert? (you ever / be)
6 I _____ my scuba diving instructor for five years. (know)

Present Perfect Continuous
We use the **Present Perfect Continuous** to talk about
- something that started in the past and is still in progress.
  Mum and Dad *have been cleaning* the house all day.
- something that started in the past and has happened repeatedly.
  The team *has been training* for the championship every day this week.
- something that happened in the past and may have finished, but it has a result in the present.
  The girls *have been studying* all night. They're exhausted.
- how long something has been happening from the past up to now.
  This athlete *has been competing* in the Winter Olympics for eight years.

Time expressions
We use the following **time expressions** with the **Present Perfect Continuous**: all day, for a long time, for (very) long, years, lately, recently, since, for.
He has been reading the newspaper *all morning*.
I haven't been living here *for very long*.

Remember! We use *for* and *since* to show the duration of an action. We've been living in this city *since* July. Josh has been watching TV *for* two hours.

Affirmative	Negative	Question	Short answers	
I've been running	I haven't been running	Have I been running …?	Yes, I have.	No, I haven't.
you've been running	you haven't been running	Have you been running …?	Yes, you have.	No, you haven't.
he's been running	he hasn't been running	Has he been running …?	Yes, he has.	No, he hasn't.
she's been running	she hasn't been running	Has she been running …?	Yes, she has.	No, she hasn't.
it's been running	it hasn't been running	Has it been running …?	Yes, it has.	No, it hasn't.
we've been running	we haven't been running	Have we been running …?	Yes, we have.	No, we haven't.
you've been running	you haven't been running	Have you been running …?	Yes, you have.	No, you haven't.
they've been running	they haven't been running	Have they been running …?	Yes, they have.	No, they haven't.

2 Complete the sentences with the Present Perfect Continuous. Use these words.

create   make   not learn   perform   play   practise

1 Daniel _has been playing_ chess for six years.
2 _____ you _____ your own blog since last month?
3 The children _____ a lot of progress at school this year.
4 Sebastian _____ English for very long.
5 _____ you _____ with the tennis champion?
6 Julie is a wonderful singer. She _____ since she was eighteen.

Present Perfect Simple vs Present Perfect Continuous

We use the **Present Perfect Simple** to talk about something we have done or achieved. The action is complete.
My classmates and I have finished our history project.

But we use the **Present Perfect Continuous** to talk about an action that has duration. It doesn't matter if the action has finished or not.
My little sister has been playing all afternoon.

We also use the **Present Perfect Simple** to talk about how many times an action has happened and to answer the questions **How much ...?**, **How many ...?** and **How many times ...?**
How many times have you visited Madrid?
We've visited Madrid three times.

But we use the **Present Perfect Continuous** to answer the question **How long ...?**
How long has Jason been waiting?
He has been waiting for half an hour.

3 Circle the correct words.

1. The toy company has constructed / (has been constructing) model planes for many years.
2. Sam hasn't played / hasn't been playing on the basketball team for long.
3. How long have you surfed / have you been surfing the Net?
4. Our coach has shouted / has been shouting all morning!
5. The volunteers have sold / have been selling raffle tickets since last Monday.
6. How many seashells have you collected / have you been collecting?

4 Complete the questions with the Present Perfect Simple or the Present Perfect Continuous using the words in brackets. Then write short answers.

1. _Have you found_ tickets for the concert yet? (you / find) ✓   _Yes, I have._
2. _____ to fix this remote control all afternoon? (Harry / try) ✗   _____
3. _____ since eleven o'clock this morning? (they / wait) ✓   _____
4. _____ their model planes for long? (the children / fly) ✗   _____
5. _____ her studies? (your sister / finish) ✗   _____
6. _____ all its milk? (the baby / drink) ✓   _____

5 Rewrite the sentences using the words given. Use between two and five words.

1. I met Sarah six years ago and we are still friends.
   I _have known Sarah for_ six years. **known**
2. We started jogging three hours ago and we are still jogging.
   We _____ three hours. **been**
3. Tommy scored three goals and the match isn't over.
   Tommy _____ three times so far in the match. **has**
4. My parents visited Rome in 1998, 2007 and 2009.
   My parents _____ three times. **visited**
5. You started sailing at six o'clock this morning and you are still on the lake!
   _____ since six o'clock this morning. **have**
6. Sandra used to collect posters but she doesn't anymore.
   Sandra _____ posters recently. **been**

6 Complete the telephone conversation with the Present Perfect Simple or the Present Perfect Continuous. Use the words in brackets.

Millie: Joe, I can't talk now. I've got to get ready for my rounders match.
Joe: Rounders? What's that?
Millie: (1) _Haven't you heard_ (you / not hear) of rounders? It's a sport. School children (2) _____ (play) it since the 15th century and it (3) _____ (always be) especially popular with girls.
Joe: Oh, I see. What do you have to do?
Millie: Well, you have to hit a small hard ball with a bat and then run round the pitch.
Joe: It sounds like baseball.
Millie: Yes, it's also similar to cricket. For years schools (4) _____ (hold) competitions. It's fun.
Joe: Mm. I (5) _____ (never be) keen on cricket, or baseball. They're too boring for me.
Millie: Well, my team (6) _____ (practise) for weeks now. The big match is today and we (7) _____ (ever not beat) our rivals.
Joe: Good luck then!
Millie: Thanks!

Speaking

Imagine that you have arranged a surprise party for a friend. Talk with your partner about what preparations have been made. Use the Present Perfect Simple, the Present Perfect Continuous and the suggestions to help you.

- order a birthday cake
- decorate the room
- lay out the food
- arrange tables and chairs
- select CDs

I have bought the soft drinks.

My mum has made pizza and hamburgers.

Lesson 2
Relative Clauses

Relative Clauses

We use **relative clauses** to give more information about people, animals, places and things. A **relative clause** begins with a **relative pronoun** (who, whom, which, whose) or a **relative adverb** (when, where, why).
We use
- **who** for people.
  There's the runner who broke the world record.
- **whom** for people.
  They chose the boy whom I had recommended.
- **whose** to say that something belongs to someone.
  There's the boy whose bike was stolen.
- **which** for animals and things.
  Where's the cafè which makes yummy milkshakes?
- **where** for places.
  That's the store where I buy my shoes.
- **when** for the time something happens.
  Do you remember the day when we got lost?
- **why** for the reason something happened.
  Do you know the reason why Janet is ignoring me?

We can use **whom** for people when the relative pronoun refers to the object of the sentence. However, it isn't usually used in everyday speech.

The diving instructor whom I spoke to was very friendly.
The diving instructor (that/who) I spoke to was very friendly.

When there is a preposition before the relative pronoun, we must use **whom** and not **who**.
The diving instructor to whom I spoke was very friendly.

A relative adverb can be used instead of a preposition and a relative pronoun.
When can replace **in / on which**
Where can replace **in / at which**
Why can replace **for which**
December is the month in which he celebrates his birthday.
December is the month when he celebrates his birthday.

1 Complete the sentences with who, whom, which, whose, where, when or why.

1 There's the guide _____who_____ speaks many languages.
2 Do you remember the magician _____ tricks were very dangerous?
3 Is Lucy the girl to _____ you tell your secrets?
4 Name the river _____ flows through central London.
5 My cousin doesn't remember the year _____ she went to London.
6 I don't understand the reason _____ people enjoy extreme sports.
7 We participate in activities _____ are for adventurous types.
8 Can we visit the National Park _____ we saw the huge waterfall?

Defining Relative Clauses

Defining relative clauses give essential information about a person, animal, place or thing that we are referring to. Without this information, the sentence doesn't make sense. We don't use commas in **defining relative clauses**.
There's the player who scored the goal.
I visited the school where my mum used to go.

In a **defining relative clause**, we can use **that** instead of **who** or **which**.
The student who/that won the scholarship is my cousin.
The dog which/that ran onto the tennis court was Nancy's.

We don't need to use a **relative pronoun** (**who, which** or **that**) when it refers to the object of the **defining relative clause**.
Jonathan is the boy who they chose as captain of the baseball team.
Jonathan is the boy they chose as captain of the baseball team.

---

2 Circle the correct words.

1 The hobby **which** / who I took up isn't very interesting.
2 Is that the sports centre **where** / **which** you go bowling?
3 The sports car **who** / **-** I like is very expensive.
4 Let's go to the pool **which** / **where** I go diving.
5 Show me the girl **who** / **whose** father is a film star.
6 I can't remember the day **when** / **where** we went to the beach.
7 The song **when** / **that** won the competition is great.
8 Tell me the reason **why** / **which** you don't want to come to my party.

Non-defining relative clauses

Non-defining relative clauses give extra information about the person, animal, place or thing that we are referring to. This information isn't necessary for the sentence to make sense and it is separated from the rest of the sentence with commas.
The new adventure park, which has many exciting rides, is very close to my house.
The track and field athlete, who won the 100-metre race, is visiting our school next week.

In a **non-defining relative clause**, we can't use **that** instead of **who** or **which**.

We can't omit the **relative pronoun** (**who, which** or **that**) in a **non-defining relative clause** even if it refers to the object of the **relative clause**.

3 Underline the non-defining relative clauses and circle the defining relative clauses.
1 There's the girl (who told me about the new rules.)
2 The famous singer, who has received three gold records, is signing autographs.
3 The naughty twins, whose parents are forever shouting, have just broken their neighbour's window.
4 Can you help the children who are having difficulty with English?
5 The golf club, at which Mum and Dad play golf with their friends, has many famous members.
6 London is the place where the 2012 Olympic Games will take place.

4 Combine the sentences using the words in bold.
1 Max is a great tennis player. He has won many trophies. **who**
   Max, who has won many trophies, is a great tennis player/Max, who is a great tennis player, has won many trophies.
2 Nicola sings in a rock band. She is my next-door neighbour. **who**

3 My uncle Robert drives a sports car. His favourite pastime is racing. **whose**

4 The 2004 Olympic Games took place in Athens. They were a great success. **which**

5 Timothy is my little brother. I give him all my old clothes. **whom**

6 Notting Hill is an area in London. The film *Notting Hill* was shot there. **where**

5 Cross out **that**, **which** or **who** where possible.
1 Is that the gorge ~~that~~ Peter was telling us about?
2 Those children, who are white water rafting, are very reckless.
3 The play which we saw last night was so boring!
4 There's the rucksack that I've been looking for!
5 I interviewed the writer that had won the Nobel prize in Literature.
6 I often read books which are about health and fitness.

6 Complete the text. Use these words.

| ~~when~~ | where | which | who | whose | why |

1966 was the year (1) _____when_____ England won the World Cup. On the day of the final, 98,000 people arrived at Wembley Stadium, (2) _____ the match took place. Germany was the team (3) _____ England had to play against.

The first player to celebrate was Helmut Haller, (4) _____ scored the first goal for Germany. The English fans cheered for Martin Peters, (5) _____ goal put England back in the match a little later.

A 2-2 draw at the end of 90 minutes was the reason (6) _____ the match went into extra time and in the 98th minute, Geoff Hurst scored the goal that everybody called the 'ghost goal', as many people thought the ball didn't cross the line. He scored again in the last minute, so England finally won the World Cup Final 4-2.

7 Rewrite the sentences using the words given. Use between two and five words.

1 Olga doesn't like risky sports. That's why she doesn't try mountain climbing. **for**
The reason ___*for which Olga doesn't*___ try mountain climbing is that she doesn't like risky sports.

2 My teammates and I played handball in a stadium yesterday. The Olympic Games had taken place there. **where**
My teammates and I played handball in a stadium _____ taken place.

3 Do you know the actor? They presented an award to him. **to**
Do you know the actor _____ an award?

4 Jenson Button won the F1 championship in 2009. I remember that day! **when**
I remember the _____ Jenson Button won the F1 championship.

5 Ginnie recognised the man. His picture appeared in the newspaper. **whose**
Ginnie recognised the man _____ in the newspaper.

6 Kite surfing is my favourite sport. It isn't very common. **which**
Kite surfing, _____, isn't very common.

Speaking

Talk to your partner about these things using defining and non-defining clauses.

- a person you know well
- your favourite hobby
- the time you had a lot of fun
- some information about your mum's car
- a food you dislike
- a place you and your friends go to regularly

Tennis is the sport that I really enjoy.

Paul, who is my best friend, lives next door to our school.

Lesson 3
Too & Enough

Too & enough

We use **too + adjective** to show that there is more of something than we need or want.
Cricket is too boring for me.

We use **adjective + enough** to show that there is as much of something as we need.
Pat is experienced enough for the job.

We can also use **enough** before uncountable nouns and plural countable nouns to show that there is as much or as many of something as we need.
There is enough cheese to make a sandwich.
There are enough contestants for the art competition.

We use **not enough** when there is less of something than we need or want.
There aren't enough glasses for everyone.
We haven't got enough money for an indoor swimming pool.

1 Complete the sentences with **too** or **enough**.

1 I'm not keen on bungee jumping, as I'm not adventurous _____enough_____ .
2 We don't want to go out. We're _____ tired.
3 Have you got _____ players for the Cup Final?
4 Rosie doesn't have _____ time to take up a new sport.
5 Yoga is _____ boring for me!
6 Is Jamie fit _____ to take part in the marathon?
7 Charlie doesn't want skiing lessons. He thinks it's _____ hard.
8 I don't have _____ money to buy new trainers.

41

2 Complete the dialogue. Use these phrases.

enough time   not talented enough   not tall enough
not too late   too much homework   too strenuous

Stephan: Do you think Robbie will become a professional tennis player?
Alicia: I don't know. In my opinion, he's (1) _not talented enough_ to make it to the top.
Stephan: Really? He's always playing in tournaments though. I admire him. I haven't got (2) _____ to play in tournaments. We always have (3) _____ .
Alicia: I know. It's not easy training every day.
Stephan: And tennis is (4) _____ for me. I prefer water sports.
Alicia: What would you like to become, Stephan?
Stephan: I've always wanted to surf, but I never had time to take it up.
Alicia: Well, it's (5) _____ now. You're only 14!
Stephan: Mm, you're right. Oh, I like basketball, too.
Alicia: Sorry Stephan, you're just (6) _____ ! Basketball players are twice your height!

3 Choose the correct answers.

1 I haven't got _____ to do a project on wildlife.
   a too much information
   b enough information
   c not enough information

2 We can walk to the youth club. It's _____ .
   a too far
   b far enough
   c close enough

3 Teenagers _____ these days.
   a don't have enough free time
   b enough free time
   c don't have free time too

4 Parachuting is much _____ . I'm not going to try it.
   a safe enough
   b too dangerous
   c dangerous enough

5 You won't be able to ski to day. There _____ on the mountains.
   a isn't enough snow
   b too much snow
   c is enough snow

6 You're so tall now. Your trousers _____ for you.
   a are long enough
   b aren't too long
   c aren't long enough

7 Oliver wants to keep fit, but he _____ to join a gym.
   a isn't old enough
   b isn't too old
   c isn't enough old

8 Just be patient! There _____ balloons for everyone.
   a aren't enough
   b are enough
   c not enough

9 There are _____ people in front of me. I can't see who's winning the race!
   a aren't enough
   b enough
   c too many

10 There won't be a party at the end of the year. Unfortunately, parents _____ to help.
   a aren't willing enough
   b too willing
   c are enough willing

4 Look at the pictures and complete the sentences with **too** or **enough** and these words.

expensive   few   little   quiet   ~~warm~~   young

1 It isn't _warm enough_ to jump in the pool.

4 It isn't _____ for Mr Davids to work.

2 There are _____ ice creams for the children.

5 Sammy is _____ to take part in the archery competition.

3 Summer camp is _____ this year. We're not going to go.

6 There's _____ sugar to make a cake.

Speaking

Imagine your seven-year-old brother wants to take up windsurfing and you think that he shouldn't. Talk with your partner about what you would tell him. Use too and enough and these suggestions to help you.

- dangerous
- tiring
- risky
- strenuous

I don't think you are old enough to take up windsurfing.

I think it's too strenuous for you.

4 Lesson 1

Past Perfect Continuous

Past Perfect Continuous

We use the **Past Perfect Continuous** to
- emphasise the duration of an action that was in progress before another action or time in the past.
  I *had been waiting* for Jane for half an hour before she finally arrived.
- talk about an action that was in progress in the past which affected a later action or state.
  Our neighbours *had been making* a lot of noise so we finally called the police.

We form the affirmative with **had been** and the main verb with the ending **–ing**.
Jennifer *had been shopping* for hours before she went home.

In the negative form we use **hadn't been** and the main verb with the ending **–ing**.
Paul *hadn't been working* for very long when he got a promotion.

In the question form we use **had been** and the main verb with the ending **–ing**. In short answers we only use **had**. We don't use the main verb.
Had you *been watching* TV all evening before you went to bed?
Yes, I *had*.

Time expressions
We use the following **time expressions** with the **Past Perfect Continuous**: all day, for weeks/ages/a (very) long time, since four o'clock, at the time.

Affirmative	Negative	Question	Short answers	
I had been running you had been running he had been running she had been running it had been running we had been running you had been running they had been running	I hadn't been running you hadn't been running he hadn't been running she hadn't been running it hadn't been running we hadn't been running you hadn't been running they hadn't been running	Had I been running …? Had you been running …? Had he been running …? Had she been running …? Had it been running …? Had we been running …? Had you been running …? Had they been running …?	Yes, I had. Yes, you had. Yes, he had. Yes, she had. Yes, it had. Yes, we had. Yes, you had. Yes, they had.	No, I hadn't. No, you hadn't. No, he hadn't. No, she hadn't. No, it hadn't. No, we hadn't. No, you hadn't. No, they hadn't.

1 Complete the sentences with the Past Perfect Continuous. Use the verbs in brackets.

1. Billy _had been working_ on a farm before he moved to the city. (work)
2. Marcia _____ all night before she saw the urban lights of the city. (drive)
3. I _____ on the rooftop for very long when it started to rain! (not sit)
4. We _____ the hospital for two hours before the ambulance finally arrived. (phone)
5. Tim and Wendy _____ tennis for long when Wendy hurt her leg. (not play)
6. Our headmaster _____ about the pros and cons of exams all morning when there was a sudden power cut. (talk)

2 Look at the pictures and complete the sentences with the correct form of the Past Perfect Continuous. Use these verbs.

argue   rely   show   study   talk   wait

1. Grandma _hadn't been waiting_ for a long time when the bus arrived.
4. Mum _____ me how to use my new mobile phone just before Dad came home.

2. The girls _____ about what colour to paint their room before they agreed to paint it yellow.
5. Gemma fell asleep during the test because she _____ all night!

3. Joe _____ on his parents to drive him everywhere before he passed his driving test.
6. Kerry and Lily finally made up. They _____ for weeks!

3 **Complete the questions with the Past Perfect Continuous and the words in brackets. Then complete the short answers.**

1 _Had you been walking_ the dog before I arrived? (you / walk)
 Yes, _I had_ .
2 _____ in the city hall before he became a teacher? (Jack / work)
 No, _____ .
3 _____ in the fields when she found the stray cat? (Teresa / cycle)
 Yes, _____ .
4 _____ at Reading University before you moved to Manchester? (you / study)
 No, _____ .
5 _____ for a long time before she opened the door? (Clare's classmates / knock)
 Yes, _____ .

4 **Complete the dialogue with the Past Perfect Continuous. Use the verbs in brackets.**

Freddie: How was your summer in New York?
Alice: Good.
Freddie: Good? You (1) _had been talking_ (talk) about it day and night before you left!
Alice: I know. The truth is, I (2) _____ (look forward to) it for ages. I (3) _____ (not think) about anything else.
Freddie: I remember! And for a very long time, your cousin Trish (4) _____ (boast) about how big her college was and how great life was in New York.
Alice: Mm.
Freddie: So, isn't life great in The Big Apple?
Alice: Well, it is. New York is amazing. It's absolutely beautiful, with many historic sites, museums and beautiful parks. I (5) _____ (dream) of walking through Central Park for years!
Freddie: So?
Alice: It made me realise how lucky we are to live in the countryside.
Freddie: I know. Trish doesn't think so though, does she? Before she went to the States, she (6) _____ (complain) about how dull country life is.
Alice: You're right! Trish loves it there.

 Speaking

Look at these pictures with you partner. Talk about what the children had been doing when the storm struck.

Some boys had been playing football when the storm struck.

These girls had been playing tennis when the storm struck.

Lesson 2

Past Perfect Simple & Past Perfect Simple vs Past Perfect Continuous

Past Perfect Simple

We use the **Past Perfect Simple** to talk about
- something that happened in the past before another action in the past.
  I *had set* the security alarm before I left home.
- something that happened before a specific time in the past. We often use the word **by** to mean *before* or *not later than*.
  By ten o'clock yesterday morning, we *had done* our shopping.
- something that happened in the past and had an effect on a later action.
  Julie *had won* a lot of money so she decided to buy an apartment in the city centre.

See the list of past participles on page 159.

Time expressions
We use the following **time expressions** with the **Past Perfect Simple**: after, already, as soon as, before, by (time or date), just, when.
Janet had just sat down when the phone rang.
Brian had already handed in his assignment.

Affirmative	Negative	Question	Short answers	
I had found	I hadn't found	Had I found ...?	Yes, I had.	No, I hadn't.
you had found	you hadn't found	Had you found ...?	Yes, you had.	No, you hadn't.
he had found	he hadn't found	Had he found ...?	Yes, he had.	No, he hadn't.
she had found	she hadn't found	Had she found ...?	Yes, she had.	No, she hadn't.
it had found	it hadn't found	Had it found ...?	Yes, it had.	No, it hadn't.
we had found	we hadn't found	Had we found ...?	Yes, we had.	No, we hadn't.
you had found	you hadn't found	Had you found ...?	Yes, you had.	No, you hadn't.
they had found	they hadn't found	Had they found ...?	Yes, they had.	No, they hadn't.

1 Complete the sentences with the Past Perfect Simple. Use the verbs in brackets.

1. When I arrived home, I realised I ___had forgotten___ my bag on the bus. (forget)
2. Mandy felt terrible because she _____ all night. (not sleep)
3. I only understood the movie because I _____ the book. (read)
4. As soon as I _____ the room, my mum called me back. (leave)
5. Sebastian _____ the car when it started to rain. (just wash)
6. Tim _____ the question until Mr Jones explained it to him. (not understand)

2 Write questions.

1. ___Had you fallen asleep by 10 o'clock last night?___
   Yes, I had fallen asleep by 10 o'clock last night.
2. _____
   No, Christine hadn't stayed on a farm before.
3. _____
   Yes, our grandparents had lived in Ireland before we were born.
4. _____
   No, they hadn't eaten all the ice cream before I arrived.
5. _____
   Yes, I had just moved house when I met Sue.
6. _____
   Yes, I had already replied to his email.

Past Perfect Simple vs Past Perfect Continuous
We use both the **Past Perfect Simple** and **Past Perfect Continuous** to talk about actions that happened in the past before another past action.
Natalie *had finished* her project before she went out.
We *had been waiting* for ages before the doctor arrived.

However, we use the **Past Perfect Continuous** to emphasise how long the first action was in progress for.
My classmates and I *had been raising* money for stray animals for a very long time.

We also use the **Past Perfect Continuous** to show that we don't know whether the action was completed or not.
Jason *had been exercising*, so he was tired.

---

3 Circle the correct words.

1. Before we moved to the city, my family and I **had always liked** / had always been liking living in the suburbs.
2. I had studied / had been studying at the library all morning when I decided to take a break.
3. My classmates and I hadn't noticed / hadn't been noticing the adventure playground before Dad showed it to us.
4. Before I joined the local gym, I hadn't realised / hadn't been realising how important exercise is.
5. The children were exhausted because they had swum / had been swimming all afternoon.
6. The dog had dug / had been digging all morning before it finally found its bone.

4 Look at the pictures and complete the sentences with the correct form of the Past Perfect Simple or the Past Perfect Continuous. Use these verbs.

~~depart~~   do   leave   miss   train   watch

1 When Tom got to the station the train _had departed_ .

2 Mandy realised how much she _____ the peace and quiet of the countryside.

3 Dad was very tired at lunch. He _____ the gardening all morning.

4 Josh was angry as his little brother _____ him any biscuits.

5 Marcus was exhausted because he _____ all morning.

6 The children _____ a documentary before they wrote a report.

5 Complete the diary entry with the Past Perfect Simple or the Past Perfect Continuous. Use the verbs in brackets.

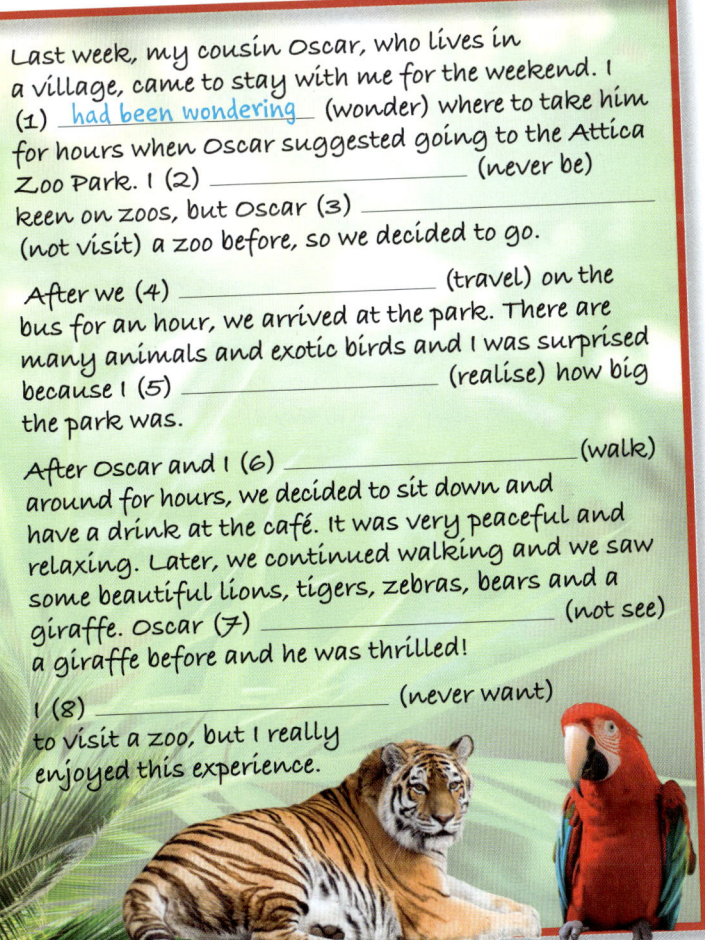

Last week, my cousin Oscar, who lives in a village, came to stay with me for the weekend. I (1) _had been wondering_ (wonder) where to take him for hours when Oscar suggested going to the Attica Zoo Park. I (2) _____ (never be) keen on zoos, but Oscar (3) _____ (not visit) a zoo before, so we decided to go.

After we (4) _____ (travel) on the bus for an hour, we arrived at the park. There are many animals and exotic birds and I was surprised because I (5) _____ (realise) how big the park was.

After Oscar and I (6) _____ (walk) around for hours, we decided to sit down and have a drink at the café. It was very peaceful and relaxing. Later, we continued walking and we saw some beautiful lions, tigers, zebras, bears and a giraffe. Oscar (7) _____ (not see) a giraffe before and he was thrilled!

I (8) _____ (never want) to visit a zoo, but I really enjoyed this experience.

Speaking

Tom had lots of things to do before he went on holiday. Look at his list below and talk to you partner about what he had and hadn't done before he left for the airport.

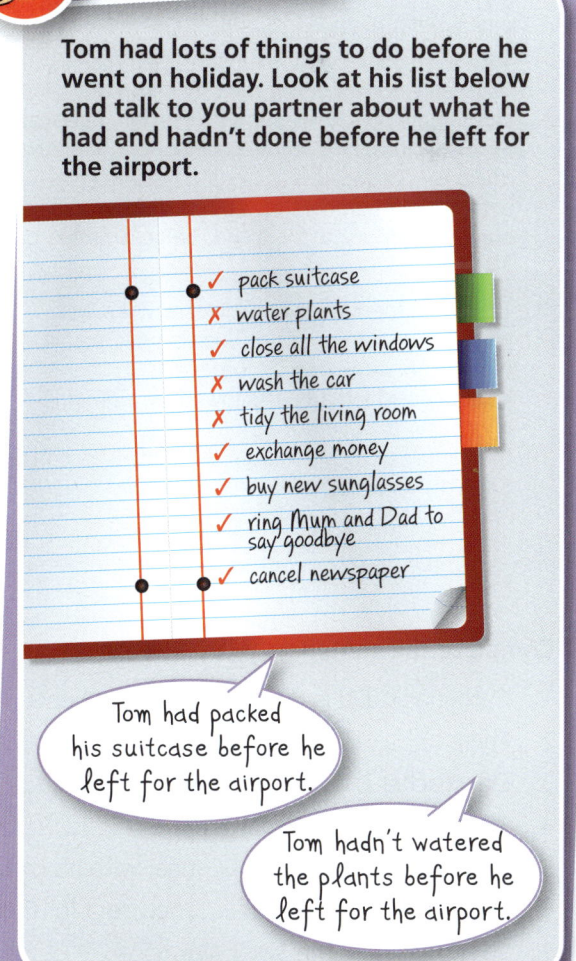

✓ pack suitcase
✗ water plants
✓ close all the windows
✗ wash the car
✗ tidy the living room
✓ exchange money
✓ buy new sunglasses
✓ ring Mum and Dad to say goodbye
✓ cancel newspaper

Tom had packed his suitcase before he left for the airport.

Tom hadn't watered the plants before he left for the airport.

4 Lesson 3
Articles

The Indefinite Article
We use the **indefinite articles a / an**
- with a singular countable noun when we mention it for the first time.
  This is an amazing adventure park.
- with a singular countable noun when making a general statement.
  You don't need a car in the city centre.
- with nouns which refer to professions, nationalities or religions.
  Mr Greenhalf is a French teacher.
  Philip is an American.
- with certain numbers instead of **one**, and some quantifying phrases such as: **a thousand**, **twice a week**, **once an hour** etc.
  Mum drives to work once a week.

We don't use the indefinite articles **a / an** with
- plural countable nouns or uncountable nouns.
  We always drink milk for breakfast.
- adjectives which aren't followed by a noun.
  My cousin is adventurous!
- the names of meals, unless there is an adjective before them.
  Can you come to my house for dinner?
  Mum cooked a lovely meal last night.

Remember!
When a word begins with a vowel, but the vowel sounds like a consonant in the word, we use **a**.
Jennifer is a university graduate.
When a word begins with a consonant, but the consonant sounds like a vowel in the word, we use **an**.
I want to buy an MP4 player.

1 Complete the sentences with a, an or -.

1. Catherine's dad is ___an___ architect.
2. There's _____ great funfair just outside the city centre.
3. Our teacher is going to take us out for _____ lunch.
4. The flight to Paris is approximately _____ hour long.
5. Dad takes _____ sugar with his coffee.
6. I really need _____ new sofa for the living room.
7. We go skiing in the Swiss Alps once _____ year.
8. William wrote _____ interesting story.

The Definite Article

We use the **definite article the**
- with singular and plural countable and uncountable nouns to talk about something specific or when we mention something for a second time.
  Can you pass me the salt, please?
  Mum bought me a T-shirt. The T-shirt is really cool.
- before unique nouns, names of hotels, cinemas, theatres and musical instruments.
  We haven't seen the sun for three days because it's been raining!
  Are you staying at the Marriott Hotel?
  Melina plays the trumpet.
- for historical periods or events.
  At the moment, we're learning about the Cold War.
- for groups of islands, mountain ranges, rivers and deserts.
  We're renting a house on one of the Greek islands.
  Kate is doing a project on the Sahara Desert.
- before superlatives.
  This is the most beautiful view I've ever seen.
- before nationalities.
  I'm very keen on the Spanish.
- with dates and with the words **morning, afternoon, evening** and **night**.
  Amy was born on the 6th of November.
- with adjectives referring to a group of people.
  We really should help the homeless more.

We don't use the **definite article** with
- proper nouns.
  James is a talented table tennis player.
- the names of sports, games, colours, days, months, holidays, subjects of study and languages (not followed by the word **language**).
  Kylie plays ice-hockey for the national team.
  Luke speaks French. (But Luke speaks the French language.)
- names of most countries (but the USA, the Netherlands), cities, streets (but the High Street), parks, bridges, islands, lakes and continents.
  Marcus was born in Thailand.
  We'll meet you at the cafè on Bond Street.
- with the words **church, school, hospital, prison, university** when they are used as a general term.
  Helen's been at university for two years.

2 Complete the sentences with **the** or **–**.

1 My grandparents moved to ___the___ United States after ___the___ Second World War.
2 Every year, Elisa travels to _____ Sweden.
3 _____ Saturday is my favourite day or the week.
4 Is _____ head teacher at your school Australian?
5 This is _____ most spectacular concert I've ever been to!
6 We went on a boat trip along _____ River Nile.
7 Many people can speak _____ English language.
8 I used to love playing _____ hide-and-seek.

3 Complete the text with **a, an, the** or **–**.

Mount Olympus is (1) ___the___ highest mountain in Greece and one of (2) _____ tallest mountains in (3) _____ Europe. It is located on (4) _____ borders of Thessaly and Macedonia, and it is about 100 km away from (5) _____ Thessaloniki, (6) _____ Greece's second largest city. In Greek mythology, Mount Olympus was (7) _____ home of the Gods. Nowadays, you can go on (8) _____ trips up the mountain. About 10,000 people climb (9) _____ mountain every year to enjoy (10) _____ amazing view.

4 Circle the correct words.

1 We're going backpacking around Greek Islands / **the Greek Islands** this summer.
2 Have you ever seen an eagle / eagle?
3 At the moment, we are learning about the Battle of Trafalgar / Battle of Trafalgar in history.
4 We have raised a large amount of money to help the poor / poor.
5 We had a beautiful breakfast / beautiful breakfast on the roof garden.
6 The new blockbuster thriller is on at Orion Cinema / the Orion Cinema.

5 The words in bold are wrong. Write - or the correct words.

1 Let's go to **a** new shopping mall this afternoon. It's just opened!   *the*
2 These are **a** worst living conditions I have ever seen.
3 My parents and I are travelling to **the** Lake Como for Christmas.
4 Can you come to our country house for **the** lunch next Sunday?
5 This is **the** very nice violin.
6 Nick graduated from university and he became **the** lawyer.

Talk to your partner about what you know about these places.

Everest
The River Nile
Adventure Park
Santorini
New York
Barcelona
Library
The Alps
The Zoo

Mount Everest is the tallest mountain in the world.

Barcelona is a city in Spain.

Units 3 & 4

1 Complete the sentences with the Present Perfect Simple. Use these verbs.

be   buy   give   protect   take part   visit

1 I _____have_____ never _____visited_____ such a picturesque village before!
2 My classmates and I _____ in three competitions this year.
3 WWF _____ always _____ endangered species.
4 My grandparents _____ just _____ a new apartment near the botanical gardens.
5 You _____ in the adventure park since 11 o'clock this morning! Aren't you tired?
6 The government _____ our local community some money for bicycle lanes.

2 Complete this text with the Present Perfect Continuous. Use the verbs in brackets.

My family and I (1) __have been looking for__ (look for) a cottage in Devon, but they all seem to be very expensive. We chose Devon because we (2) _____ (spend) our weekends there for years now.

We all like peaceful weekends away from the hustle and bustle of the city centre. Dad and Joe, my brother, enjoy walking and for the past three years, they (3) _____ (trek) with a group of people from the area. We (4) _____ (argue) about where to buy this cottage, as Dad, Mum and Joe want to be near the hills but my sister and I (5) _____ (hope) to find a house nearer to the sea. We enjoy swimming and water sports. My sister (6) _____ (dive) since she was very young and I (7) _____ (sail) for two years.

At the moment, we can't find anything, so we (8) _____ (stay) in a little hotel. I hope we find something soon.

3 Complete the dialogue with the Present Perfect Simple or the Present Perfect Continuous. Use the verbs in brackets.

Rosie: Billy, I think we (1) _____have_____ finally _____found_____ (find) a solution for homeless people in our community.
Billy: Really? That's great. We (2) _____ (try) for so long!
Rosie: I spoke to the mayor and he (3) _____ (agree) to provide money for a shelter. He also wants to encourage residents to raise money for homeless people.
Billy: We (4) _____ (disagree) about this issue for the past year. Why (5) _____ he suddenly _____ (decide) to help?
Rosie: For a very long time, many people (6) _____ (complain) about the number of people living on the streets. I think he (7) _____ finally _____ (realise) how serious the problem is. We're meeting later on to discuss how to raise money.
Billy: I'll come, too. We (8) _____ (worry) about this problem for ages!

4 The words in bold are wrong. Write the correct words.

1 This house, **where** has got a rooftop garden, is extremely expensive.   _____which_____
2 That's the girl **whom** won the scholarship to study abroad.   _____
3 The botanical garden, **which** there is a huge variety of tropical plants, is on the outskirts of the city.   _____
4 Can you please tell me the time **which** the library opens?   _____
5 I know the lady **that** son owns a pet tarantula.   _____
6 The sports centre, in **where** there'll be many new facilities, should open by the end of the year.   _____

53

Review 2

Units 3 & 4

5 Choose the correct answers.

1 Sam is _____ to go to the sports centre.
   a enough tired
   b too tired ✓
   c tired enough

2 I'm not keen on the inner city. It's just _____ for me.
   a noisy enough
   b too noisy
   c enough noisy

3 There aren't any big animals in the country park. It is _____ .
   a not large enough
   b too large
   c small enough

4 My neighbourhood is dull as there _____ .
   a aren't enough facilities
   b are too many facilities
   c are enough facilities

5 You'll easily get into the local university. You're _____ .
   a too clever
   b clever enough
   c not clever enough

6 This river is _____ to swim in. Let's go to the swimming pool.
   a polluted enough
   b enough polluted
   c too polluted

6 Complete the sentences with the Past Perfect Continuous.

1 Rosie and Clare _had been talking_ during yesterday's lesson so they didn't hear about today's test. (talk)
2 _____ for long when the coach arrived? (you / practise)
3 The local community _____ a new library before they ran out of money. (construct)
4 We were exhausted last night. We _____ the gardening all afternoon. (do)
5 _____ for long before he found his way out of the maze? (Johnny / walk)
6 Mum _____ for long before Dad got home. (not cook)

7 Circle the correct words.

1 Before last night, I hadn't watched / hadn't been watching a 3D movie on TV.
2 We had hiked / had been hiking all morning when we finally saw a café.
3 Had Mr Terry taught / Had Mr Terry been teaching for years before he decided to retire?
4 Until I saw Max bungee jump off the bridge, I had never wanted / had never been wanting to try it myself.
5 Mrs Robinson had never realised / had never been realising how dull her lessons were.
6 Harriet and James got home late. They had sold / had been selling raffle tickets all evening.

8 Complete the article with a, an, the or -.

Pilates

If you want to strengthen your muscles, pilates is (1) _a_ great idea. It is (2) _____ system of physical fitness, which has improved (3) _____ lives of people of all ages all over (4) _____ world.
People started practising (5) _____ pilates in (6) _____ early twentieth century, when (7) _____ gymnast, Joseph Pilates, invented the system. His aim was to unite our body and mind, and therefore (8) _____ lot of concentration is required.
(9) _____ basic aim of pilates is to help you breathe properly and strengthen your muscles, making you feel healthier all round.
It really is worth (10) _____ try, so why not give it a go!

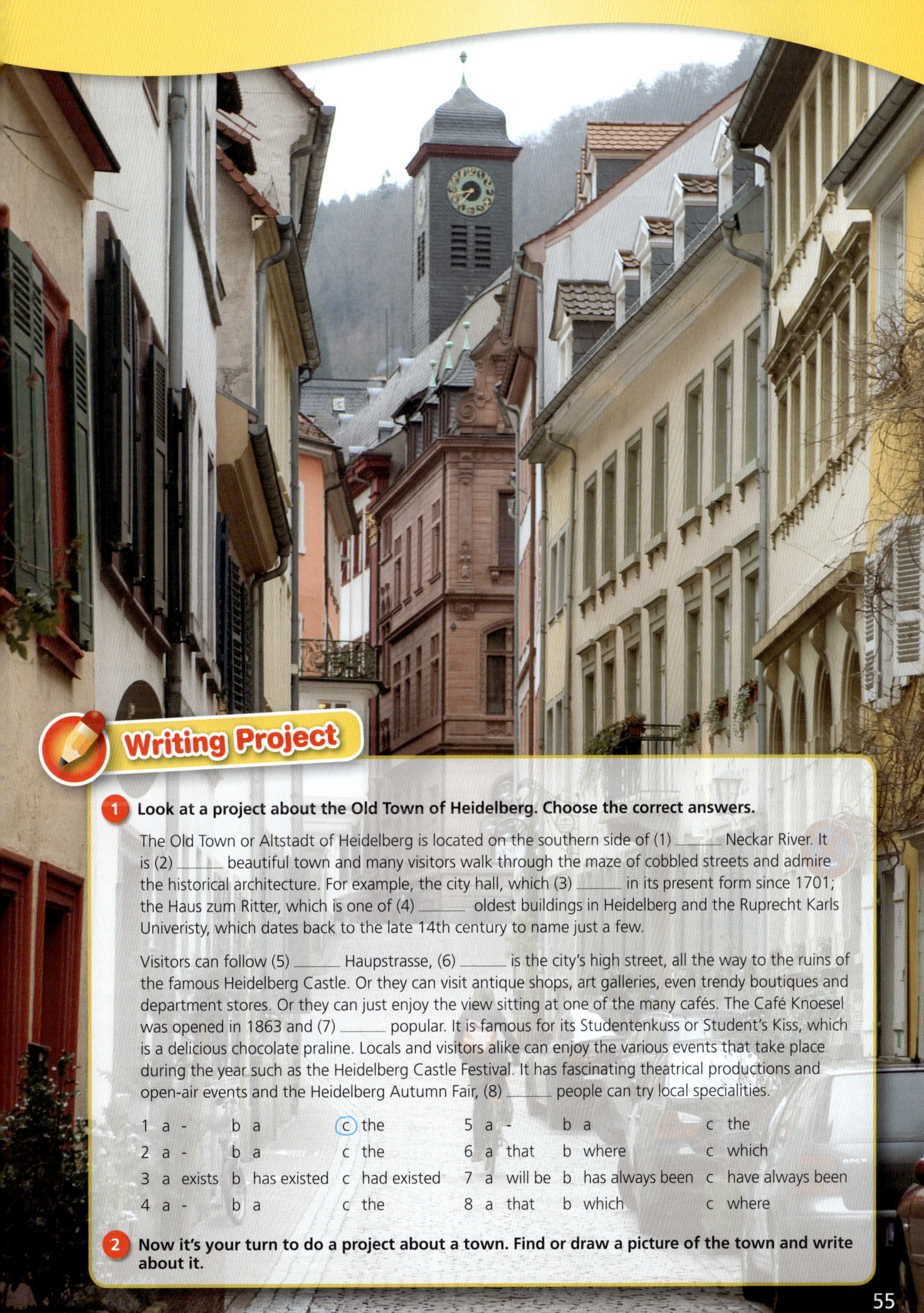

Writing Project

1 Look at a project about the Old Town of Heidelberg. Choose the correct answers.

The Old Town or Altstadt of Heidelberg is located on the southern side of (1) _____ Neckar River. It is (2) _____ beautiful town and many visitors walk through the maze of cobbled streets and admire the historical architecture. For example, the city hall, which (3) _____ in its present form since 1701; the Haus zum Ritter, which is one of (4) _____ oldest buildings in Heidelberg and the Ruprecht Karls Univeristy, which dates back to the late 14th century to name just a few.

Visitors can follow (5) _____ Haupstrasse, (6) _____ is the city's high street, all the way to the ruins of the famous Heidelberg Castle. Or they can visit antique shops, art galleries, even trendy boutiques and department stores. Or they can just enjoy the view sitting at one of the many cafés. The Café Knoesel was opened in 1863 and (7) _____ popular. It is famous for its Studentenkuss or Student's Kiss, which is a delicious chocolate praline. Locals and visitors alike can enjoy the various events that take place during the year such as the Heidelberg Castle Festival. It has fascinating theatrical productions and open-air events and the Heidelberg Autumn Fair, (8) _____ people can try local specialities.

1 a -	b a	c **the**	5 a -	b a	c the
2 a -	b a	c the	6 a that	b where	c which
3 a exists	b has existed	c had existed	7 a will be	b has always been	c have always been
4 a -	b a	c the	8 a that	b which	c where

2 Now it's your turn to do a project about a town. Find or draw a picture of the town and write about it.

Lesson 1

Future Simple, Be going to & Future Continuous

Future Simple
We use the **Future Simple** to
- talk about predictions.
  It'll be a long and tiring journey.
- talk about decisions we make at the time of speaking.
  I'll go to the bakery and buy some bread.
- talk about offers, promises, threats or warnings.
  You must be hungry. I'll make you a sandwich.
- to ask someone to do something for us.
  Will you call Jane for me, please?
- talk about opinions for the future usually after **think, hope, be sure, believe, bet** and **probably**.
  I'm sure Brian will pass with flying colours.

Note that we use **shall** with **I** or **we** in questions when we want to offer to do something or suggest something.
Shall I make you a milkshake?

Time expressions
We use the following **time expressions** with the **Future Simple**: **tomorrow, in the morning/afternoon/evening, this week/weekend/month/year, in a week/month/year**, etc.
I'll take the dog for a walk in the afternoon.

Affirmative	Negative	Question	Short answers	
I'll help	I won't help	Will I help …?	Yes, I will.	No, I won't.
you'll help	you won't help	Will you help …?	Yes, you will.	No, you won't.
he'll help	he won't help	Will he help …?	Yes, he will.	No, he won't.
she'll help	she won't help	Will she help …?	Yes, she will.	No, she won't.
it'll help	it won't help	Will it help …?	Yes, it will.	No, it won't.
we'll help	we won't help	Will we help …?	Yes, we will.	No, we won't.
you'll help	you won't help	Will you help …?	Yes, you will.	No, you won't.
they'll help	they won't help	Will they help …?	Yes, they will.	No, they won't.

1 Complete the sentences with the correct form of the Future Simple. Use these verbs.

be   depart   give   not come   pass   stimulate

1 I'm sure the interactive whiteboard ___will stimulate___ learning.
2 _____ the flight _____ on time?
3 The weather is awful! I _____ skiing with you.
4 Do you think our trip to India _____ a voyage of discovery?
5 _____ she _____ you some advice on where to stay?
6 You're an intelligent boy. I believe you _____ your university finals.

Be going to
We use **be going to** to
- talk about future plans and intentions.
 Next summer, we're going to spend two months travelling around South America.
- predict that something is going to happen when we have proof or information.
 Juliette is on the wrong platform. She's going to get on the wrong train!

Affirmative	Negative	Question	Short answers	
I'm going to stay	I'm not going to stay	Am I going to stay ...?	Yes, I am.	No, I'm not.
you're going to stay	you aren't going to stay	Are you going to stay ...?	Yes, you are.	No, you're not.
he's going to stay	he isn't going to stay	Is he going to stay ...?	Yes, he is.	No, he isn't.
she's going to stay	she isn't going to stay	Is she going to stay ...?	Yes, she is.	No, she isn't.
it's going to stay	it isn't going to stay	Is it going to stay ...?	Yes, it is.	No, it isn't.
we're going to stay	we aren't going to stay	Are we going to stay ...?	Yes, we are.	No, we aren't.
you're going to stay	you aren't going to stay	Are you going to stay ...?	Yes, you are.	No, you aren't.
they're going to stay	they aren't going to stay	Are they going to stay ...?	Yes, they are.	No, they aren't.

Time expressions
We use the following **time expressions** with **be going to**: tomorrow, in the morning/afternoon/evening, this week/weekend, next week/month/year, in a week/month/year, etc.
Julie is going to buy a new car.

2 Complete the dialogue with the correct form of **be going to**. Use the verbs in brackets.

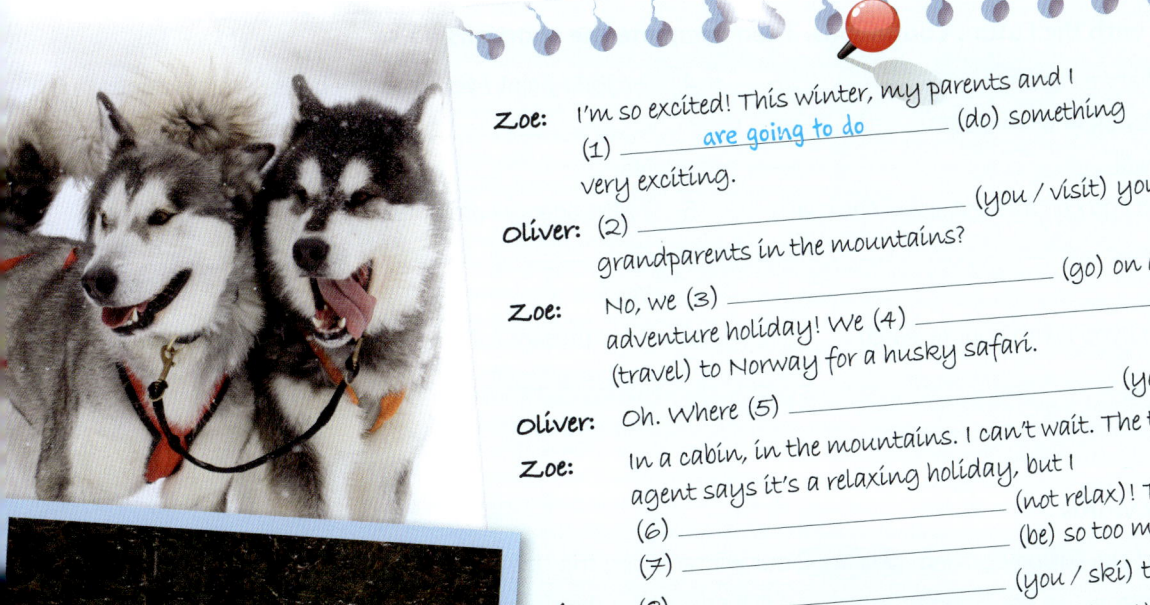

Zoe: I'm so excited! This winter, my parents and I (1) ___are going to do___ (do) something very exciting.
Oliver: (2) _____ (you / visit) your grandparents in the mountains?
Zoe: No, we (3) _____ (go) on an adventure holiday! We (4) _____ (travel) to Norway for a husky safari.
Oliver: Oh. Where (5) _____ (you / stay)?
Zoe: In a cabin, in the mountains. I can't wait. The travel agent says it's a relaxing holiday, but I (6) _____ (not relax)! There (7) _____ (be) so too much to do!
Oliver: (8) _____ (you / ski) there?
Zoe: Of course. We can go cross-country skiing through forests and along rivers. We (9) _____ (visit) a reindeer farm, too!
Oliver: It sounds great!

Future Continuous

We use the **Future Continuous**
- to talk about something that will be in progress at a specific time in the future.
  In three weeks' time, we'll be learning English at summer school.
- to ask politely about someone's future plans.
  Which cities will you be visiting during your trip around Europe?
- to talk about plans that will definitely happen because they are routine or programmed actions.
  It's Sunday today, so Sandy will be having lunch with her grandparents.

Time expressions
We use the following **time expressions** with the **Future Continuous**: in a few hours/days/weeks, in the near future, (this time) tomorrow, next week/month/year, soon, at seven o'clock tonight/tomorrow, during the weekend/summer, soon, etc.
George will be arriving soon.

Affirmative	Negative	Question	Short answers	
I'll be working	I won't be working	Will I be working …?	Yes, I will.	No, I won't.
you'll be working	you won't be working	Will you be working …?	Yes, you will.	No, you won't.
he'll be working	he won't be working	Will he be working …?	Yes, he will.	No, he won't.
she'll be working	she won't be working	Will she be working …?	Yes, she will.	No, she won't.
it'll be working	it won't be working	Will it be working …?	Yes, it will.	No, it won't.
we'll be working	we won't be working	Will we be working …?	Yes, we will.	No, we won't.
you'll be working	you won't be working	Will you be working …?	Yes, you will.	No, you won't.
they'll be working	they won't be working	Will they be working …?	Yes, they will.	No, they won't.

3 Complete the sentences with the Future Continuous. Use the verbs in brackets.

1. This time next month, we ___'ll be lying___ on a sandy beach in the Caribbean. (lie)
2. In two hours' time, you _____ your flight to South Africa. (board)
3. This time tomorrow, my classmates and I _____ the Science Museum. (visit)
4. In the near future, my family and I _____ in a remote area anymore. (not live)
5. In exactly ten minutes, we _____ the Swiss border. (cross)
6. Elisa is on holiday so she _____ in the tournament this weekend. (not take part)

4 Write questions with the Future Continuous. Then complete the short answers.

1. ? / you / stay / at / a campsite
   Will you be staying at a campsite?
   Yes, ___I will___ .
2. ? / the students / go / on their excursion / by coach
   _____
   No, _____ .
3. ? / Emily / help / you / with your research
   _____
   Yes, _____ .
4. ? / you / paint / your country house / this summer
   _____
   No, _____ .
5. ? / the agency / promote / creative holidays / this year
   _____
   Yes, _____ .
6. ? / I / present / the award / to / the travel writer
   _____
   No, _____ .

5 Circle the correct words.

1. Mum promised she will be booking / **will book** our winter skiing trip this afternoon.
2. This time tomorrow, we are going to explore / will be exploring the sights in Copenhagen.
3. Shall / Will we sign up for the course to improve our English skills?
4. My sister and I have decided that we are going to go / will be going on a cruise around the Caribbean.
5. Have a look in the atlas and you will find / will be finding a map of Mozambique.
6. The policemen found some fingerprints so they are going to arrest / be arresting the suspects.

6 Choose the correct answers.

1. Finish your homework or you _____ to Freddie's party tonight.
   a. aren't going
   b. won't go
   c. be going to go

2. In two hours' time, we _____ in our car, on the way to summer camp!
   a. will sit
   b. are going to sit
   c. will be sitting

3. _____ help me lift the suitcases into the car, please?
   a. Will you be
   b. Are you going
   c. Will you

4. Mum, what _____ when Uncle Tom and Auntie Mary arrive?
   a. we will be doing
   b. are we doing
   c. will we do

5. Jeremy made a decision last night. He _____ a flat in Toledo this summer.
   a. is going to rent
   b. will rent
   c. will renting

6. Oh no! I've got no petrol in the tank. The car _____ .
   a. is going to stop
   b. will stop
   c. will be stopping

Speaking

Imagine that you are going on holiday. Talk with your partner about what you will be doing. Use the Future Simple, **be going to**, the Future Continuous and these suggestions to help you.

play beach volley

visit interesting places

eat lots of ice-cream

relax in the sun

have fun swimming

buy souvenirs / postcards

I'll be relaxing in the sun.

I'm going to buy some souvenirs.

Lesson 2

Future Perfect Simple & Future Perfect Continuous

Future Perfect Simple

We use the **Future Perfect Simple** to talk about something that will have finished
- before something else happens.
  We'll have reached the top of the mountain before it gets dark.
- before a specific time in the future.
  I'll have finished all my exams by the summer.

See the list of past participles on page 159.

Time expressions
We use the following **time expressions** with the Future Perfect Simple: before, by seven o'clock/by now/ the weekend, by tomorrow/next week/summer, in a year's time, in ten minutes, soon, etc.
Samantha will have packed her suitcase by tomorrow.

Affirmative	Negative	Question	Short answers	
I'll have arrived	I won't have arrived	Will I have arrived ...?	Yes, I will.	No, I won't.
you'll have arrived	you won't have arrived	Will you have arrived ...?	Yes, you will.	No, you won't.
he'll have arrived	he won't have arrived	Will he have arrived ...?	Yes, he will.	No, he won't.
she'll have arrived	she won't have arrived	Will she have arrived ...?	Yes, she will.	No, she won't.
it'll have arrived	it won't have arrived	Will it have arrived ...?	Yes, it will.	No, it won't.
we'll have arrived	we won't have arrived	Will we have arrived ...?	Yes, we will.	No, we won't.
you'll have arrived	you won't have arrived	Will you have arrived ...?	Yes, you will.	No, you won't.
they'll have arrived	they won't have arrived	Will they have arrived ...?	Yes, they will.	No, they won't.

1 Look at the pictures and complete the sentences with the correct form of the Future Perfect Simple. Use these verbs.

> choose   eat   ~~iron~~   paint   repair   wash

1 By six o'clock this afternoon, Mrs Jones __will have ironed__ all the clothes.

2 It's eleven o'clock. Henry _____ the house by midday.

3 _____ he _____ my car by the end of the day?

4 Johnny _____ his dinner by eight o'clock.

5 They _____ their mum's car by the end of the day.

6 _____ she _____ the destination by midnight tonight?

Future Perfect Continuous

We use the **Future Perfect Continuous** to emphasise the duration of an activity that will be in progress before another time or event in the future.
By tomorrow morning, we'll have been trekking for three days.

We form the affirmative with **will have been** and the main verb with the ending **–ing** for all persons.
Karen will have been studying for five hours by the time she goes to bed.

In the negative form we use **won't have been** and the main verb with the ending **–ing**.
We won't have been doing our homework.

In the question form we use **will have been** and the main verb with the ending **–ing**. In short answers we only use **will**. We don't use the main verb.
Will you have been living in that house for ten years by 2015?
Yes, I will.

Note that the **Future Perfect Continuous** is rarely used in the negative or question form.

Time expressions
We use the following **time expressions** with the Future Perfect Continuous: before, by seven o'clock/by now/the weekend, by tomorrow/next week/summer, in a year's time, in ten minutes, soon, etc.
By five o'clock, I'll have been answering emails for three hours.

Affirmative	Negative	Question	Short answers	
I'll have been trying	I won't have been trying	Will I have been trying ...?	Yes, I will.	No, I won't.
you'll have been trying	you won't have been trying	Will you have been trying ...?	Yes, you will.	No, you won't.
he'll have been trying	he won't have been trying	Will he have been trying ...?	Yes, he will.	No, he won't.
she'll have been trying	she won't have been trying	Will she have been trying ...?	Yes, she will.	No, she won't.
it'll have been trying	it won't have been trying	Will it have been trying ...?	Yes, it will.	No, it won't.
we'll have been trying	we won't have been trying	Will we have been trying ...?	Yes, we will.	No, we won't.
you'll have been trying	you won't have been trying	Will you have been trying ...?	Yes, you will.	No, you won't.
they'll have been trying	they won't have been trying	Will they have been trying ...?	Yes, they will.	No, they won't.

2 Complete the sentences with the Future Perfect Continuous. Use the verbs in brackets.

1 Mum's been in the kitchen all morning. In ten minutes, she _'ll have been cooking_ for three hours! (cook)
2 By August, we _____ in Argentina for four years. (live)
3 At three o'clock, the children _____ for two hours. (ski)
4 By the end of summer, the new rock band _____ Australia for three months. (tour)
5 Penny _____ Spanish for two years by the time she goes to university. (study)
6 By the end of the decade, the local community _____ this new sports complex for three years! (build)

3 Look at the list of duties for a school fête. Complete the sentences using the Future Perfect Continuous.

Name		
Karen	sell raffle tickets	10 am – 1 pm
Lisa	sell cakes and drinks at the food stall	2 pm – 5 pm
Kerrie	help at the book stall	11 am – 4 pm
Mr Peters	take children on pony rides	10 am – 5 pm
Mrs Tate	supervising carnival rides	10 am – 5 pm
Peter and Brian	organise competitions	11 am – 4 pm

1 By one o'clock, Karen _will have been selling raffle tickets for three hours_ .
2 By three o'clock, Lisa _____ .
3 By midday, Kerrie _____ .
4 By the time the fête ends, Mr Peters _____ .
5 By five o'clock, Mrs Tate _____ .
6 By two o'clock, Peter and Brian _____ .

Future Perfect Simple vs Future Perfect Continuous
We use the **Future Perfect Simple** to emphasise that a future action will be completed and we use the **Future Perfect Continuous** to emphasise the **duration** of a future action.
By four o'clock, we'll have packed our bags.
By four o'clock, we'll have been packing our bags for two hours.

---

4 Complete the sentences with the Future Perfect Simple or the Future Perfect Continuous. Use the verbs in brackets.

1 By noon tomorrow, we _will have arrived_ at base camp. (arrive)
2 Soon, Mario _____ as captain of a cruise ship for six years. (work)
3 By August, my grandparents _____ Asia for two months. (explore)
4 In a month's time, I _____ all my final exams. (finish)
5 By summer, the annual expedition _____ . (begin)
6 We _____ for twelve hours by the time we land in Dubai. (fly)

5 Choose the correct answers.

1 We _____ the border to Mexico by seven o'clock this evening.
   a will have been crossing
   b will have crossed
   c will be crossing

2 By the time I finish the marathon, I _____ for three hours.
   a will have been walking
   b will walk
   c will have walked

3 In twenty minutes, the divers _____ for three hours.
   a are
   b will have swum
   c will have been swimming

4 I _____ this volcano for days by the time I reach the crater.
   a will have been climbing
   b will have climbed
   c have climbed

5 By Christmas, Tim _____ as a guide in the Alps for six months.
   a will have been working
   b is working
   c will have worked

6 The archaeologists _____ their research by the end of their dig.
   a are completing
   b will have been completing
   c will have completed

6 Complete the telephone conversation with the Future Perfect Simple or the Future Perfect Continuous. Use the verbs in brackets.

Alex: I'm exhausted today! By this time next week, I (1) _will have been backpacking_ (backpack) around India for six weeks!

Emily: Wow! I (2) _____ (forget) what you look like by the time you get back!

Alex: You certainly will! Elizabeth and I (3) _____ (lose) so much weight by then! We don't eat very much here.

Emily: Which places have you visited so far?

Alex: Well, we're still in Goa! In one week's time, I think we (4) _____ (explore) the whole region. It's just so beautiful.

Emily: Is it carnival time there now?

Alex: Yes, it is. The carnival lasts for another two days, so by the time it ends Elizabeth and I (5) _____ (dance) for three days!

Emily: Apart from dancing at the carnival, what else is there to do?

Alex: Goa has spectacular beaches where you can relax. There are also old churches, temples, and museums which are very interesting.

Emily: I see. Are you planning to come home soon?

Alex: Mm, yes. Soon, we (6) _____ (spend) all our money.

Emily: OK! I can't wait to see you both.

Alex: Bye!

Speaking

Talk with a partner about what you will have done and what you will have been doing by the time you're eighteen. Use these suggestions to help you.

- finish school
- learn English / French
- live at home
- play sport / musical instrument
- start work
- go abroad

I will have finished high school by the time I'm eighteen.

I will have been learning French for six years.

Lesson 3

Present Tenses (future meaning) & Future Tenses

Present Simple & Present Continuous (future meaning)

We use the **Present Simple** to talk about timetabled and programmed events in the future.
The cruise ship sails at seven o'clock in the morning.

We use the **Present Continuous** to talk about fixed future plans.
We're going on safari in Zimbabwe this summer.

1 Complete the sentences with the correct form of the Present Simple or the Present Continuous. Use the verbs in brackets.

1 Flight OA1923 to London _____departs_____ at seven o'clock in the morning. (depart)
2 What time _____ in the morning? (the bank / open)
3 I _____ to the cinema tonight because I've got too much work. (go)
4 _____ her grandparents this weekend? (Susan / visit)
5 The interstate bus timetable has changed. The bus to Boston _____ at nine o'clock anymore. (leave)
6 There's a great movie on TV later so we _____ home. (stay)

Future Simple, be going to & Future Continuous

We use the **Future Simple**
- to make predictions.
  You'll have a wonderful time in Australia.
- to talk about decisions we make at the time of speaking.
  It's really cold tonight. I'll make some soup for dinner.
- to make offers, promises, threats or to give warnings.
  Be careful! You'll hurt yourself.
  I'll make you a cup of tea.
  I'll come straight home after school.
  I'll report you to the head teacher if you're late again.
- to ask someone to do something for us.
  Will you answer the phone, please?
- to state opinions for the future after **think, hope, be sure, believe, bet** and **probably**.
  Dad believes he'll get the job.

We use **be going to**
- to talk about future plans and intentions.
  We're going to ride in a hot air balloon on Sunday.
- to predict that something is going to happen when we have proof or information.
  The pavement is very slippery. I'm going to fall over!

We use the **Future Continuous**
- to talk about something that will be in progress at a specific time in the future.
  In a month's time, Suzie will be working in her dad's office.
- to ask politely about someone's future plans.
  What time will you be interviewing the candidates?

2 Look at these situations and write what these people would say. Use the correct form of the Future Simple, **be going to** or the Future Continuous.

1. It's Friday and John and Cathy are in class and they are talking about going to the beach the next day at the same time.
   This time tomorrow, we'll be going to the beach.

2. You are hungry and you ask your friend to make you a sandwich.

3. Mum is washing the dishes when somebody knocks on the door. She asks her daughter to open the door.

4. Mr Tate is looking up at the sky. There are many dark clouds.

5. You don't know what your teacher is planning to give you for homework, but you want to find out.

6. Your best friend sees a beautiful T-shirt but she decides not to buy it.

7. You and your dad are talking about his flight to London at the same time next week.

8. You have seen *Iceberg 3* and you really enjoyed it. You are sure that your friend will too.

9. Paul isn't working at the moment but in one month's time he will be. He was offered a job in a travel agency.

10. There is a party tomorrow night. You and your best friend have been invited and you plan to go.

3 Complete the dialogue with the correct form of the verbs in brackets. Use the Present Simple, the Present Continuous, the Future Simple, be going to or the Future Continuous.

Eva: Guess what we (1) _'re going/ 're going to do_ (do) this afternoon.
Billy: I don't know!
Eva: We (2) _____ (tour) around London on a double-decker bus.
Billy: Wow! What time (3) _____ (the bus / leave)?
Eva: At four o'clock. In two hours' time, we (4) _____ (admire) the sights of London from the top of a bus!
Billy: Which sights (5) _____ (you / visit)?
Eva: Oh, Westminster, Buckingham Palace, Big Ben of course and maybe Tower Bridge. But, I'm worried it might rain.
Billy: Don't worry! There isn't a cloud in the sky. It (6) _____ (rain)! I'm sure you (7) _____ (have) a wonderful time.
Eva: I hope so! Billy, could you do something for me?
Billy: What is it?
Eva: (8) _____ (you / help) me with my homework tomorrow?

Future Perfect Simple & Future Perfect Continuous

We use the **Future Perfect Simple** to talk about an action that will have been completed before another action or before a specific time in the future.
By the time you wake up, I'll have cleaned the whole house!

We use the **Future Perfect Continuous** to talk about how long an action will have been in progress by a specific time in the future.
By midday, the local citizens will have been protesting for three hours.

---

4 Circle the correct words.

1 By the end of summer we'**ll have moved** / will have been moving to our new house.
2 There is a lot of traffic. They won't have arrived / won't have been arriving by four o'clock.
3 Will the helicopter tour have finished / have been finishing by six o'clock this evening?
4 By June, the schoolchildren will have collected / will have been collecting money for the charity for nine months.
5 Don't worry. Jane won't have waited / won't have been waiting for long by the time you arrive.
6 Will Victoria have completed / have been completing her project by five o'clock?

5 The words in bold are wrong. Write the correct words.

1 The athlete is sure he will **be breaking** the world record this year.   _break_
2 This time tomorrow, we will **have been** sailing around the Canary Islands.   _____
3 In ten years' time, the scientist will **work** on this project for fifteen years.   _____
4 The movie **start** at nine o'clock.   _____
5 Will you **finish** your homework by the time I get home tonight?   _____
6 By this time tomorrow, we will **arrive** at our destination.   _____

6 Circle the correct answers.

1 This time tomorrow, Dan and Sandy _____ in the 100-metre race.
 a are competing
 b will be competing
 c will have competed

2 The athletes _____ for ten hours by the time the marathon finishes.
 a run
 b will have run
 c will have been running

3 Hurry! The performance _____ at seven o'clock.
 a will have started
 b will have been starting
 c starts

4 I bet you _____ a wonderful time at the party.
 a are going to have
 b will have
 c will have had

5 Dad promises he _____ me a moped for my seventeenth birthday.
 a will buy
 b will have bought
 c buys

6 We have decided that we _____ in a camper van this summer.
 a aren't going to travel
 b don't travel
 c won't have been travelling

7 _____ in the swimming race next weekend?
 a Do you take part
 b Will you have taken part
 c Are you taking part

8 _____ extinct by 2010?
 a Will this species have become
 b Is this species
 c Is this species being

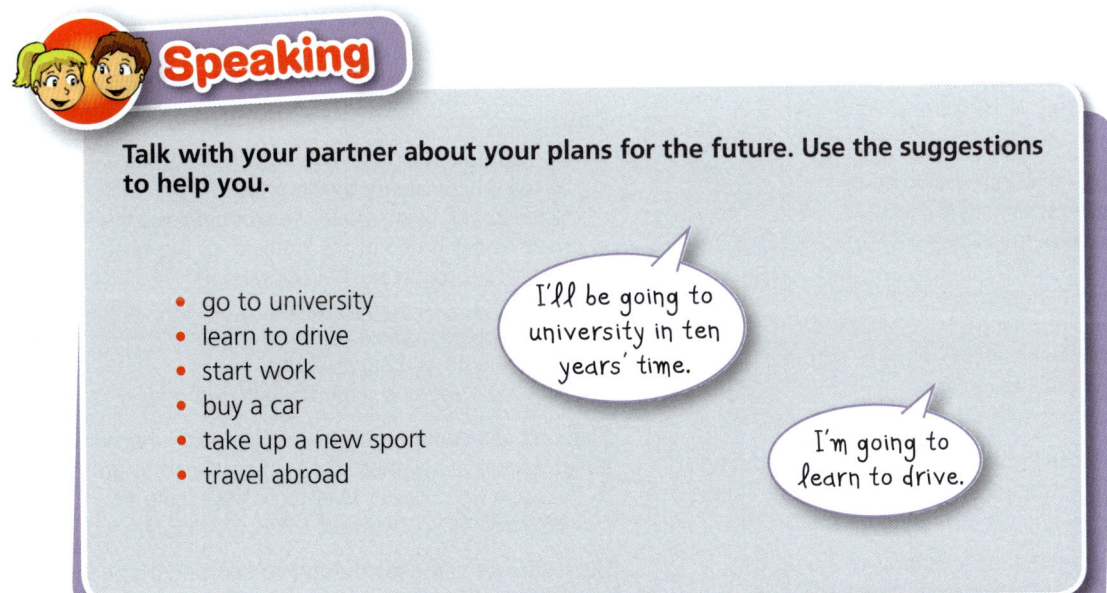

Speaking

Talk with your partner about your plans for the future. Use the suggestions to help you.

- go to university
- learn to drive
- start work
- buy a car
- take up a new sport
- travel abroad

I'll be going to university in ten years' time.

I'm going to learn to drive.

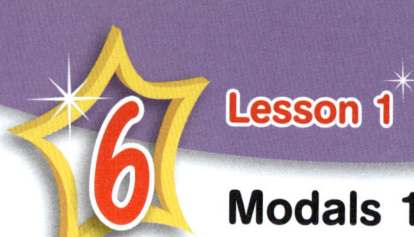

6 Lesson 1

Modals 1: Can, Could, Be able to, Would, Have to, Must & Needn't

Can

We use **can**
- to talk about ability in the present.
  Marcus can run very fast.
- to ask or give permission.
  Can I dive into the pool now?
  Yes, you can play with my DSi.
- to talk about possibility.
  We can jog around the park every morning.
- for requests and suggestions.
  Can you come with me to the doctor's, please?

We usually use **can't** instead of **cannot** in everyday English, but we sometimes use **cannot** to give emphasis.
No Susan, you cannot take all your brothers CDs!

Can is followed by the bare infinitive.
My mum can speak three foreign languages.

We often use **can** and **could** with verbs of the senses such as **see, hear, smell**, etc.
I can see the keys, they're on the kitchen table.
I could smell the spaghetti bolognaise from my bedroom!

Could

We use **could**
- to talk about ability in the past.
  Rosie could swim when she was four years old!
- to ask permission in the present or the future.
  Could I go to the park after school?
- to ask for something politely.
  Could I have a glass of water, please?
- for requests and suggestions.
  You could take up yoga to help you relax.

We don't use **could** for abilities in the past when we talk about a specific occasion when we managed to do something. In this case we use **was able to** or **were able to**.
I didn't have much time but I was able to finish my work.

However, we can use **couldn't** to talk about specific situations in the past.
I couldn't get through to Jane last night.

Could is followed by the bare infinitive.
Mrs Nichols could swim very fast when she was younger.

Remember!

Can and Could are the same for all persons.
I can sing.   I could dive.
You can sing.   You could dive.

Be able to

We use **be able to**
- to talk about ability.
  Sandra is able to speak three languages.
- to talk about a specific occasion when we managed or didn't manage to do something.
  I was able to finish all my chores today.
  (We can't use **could** here.)
  I wasn't able to start the report this morning.
  (We can also use **couldn't** here.)

We can use **be able to** with many tenses, we just use the correct form of the verb **be**. But we don't use **be able to** with continuous tenses.

Be able to is followed by the bare infinitive.
All the children were able to complete their projects on time.

---

1 Circle the correct words.

1. My grandma (could) / was able sing very well when she was younger.
2. Mrs Stevens, can I / am I able to ask you a question?
3. Sorry, I could / wasn't able to finish my project.
4. We can / are able to go to the cinema if you like.
5. Lyn is an interpreter. She can / could speak three languages.
6. I can / am able to hear you but I can't see you.

Would

We use **would** in the question form
- for requests.
  Would you help me with the cooking?
- when asking for permission.
  Would you mind if I bring a friend to the party?

We use **would** to ask more politely. When we answer a question with **would**, we use **will**.
Would you drive me home, please?
Yes, I will.

Would is followed by a noun or subject pronoun and the bare infinitive.
Would George mind if I used his phone?
Would you write down your name and address?

---

2 Complete the sentences with the correct form of **can**, **could**, **be able to**, or **would** and these verbs.

| clean | come | do | go | stay | turn off |

1. Yesterday, Mum wasn't well so she ___wasn't able to/couldn't go___ to the office.
2. _____ you _____ the computer, please?
3. I'm tired so I _____ the windows for you.
4. We _____ some stretching exercises while we are waiting for our coach to arrive.
5. _____ you and Katie _____ for a bike ride with me?
6. Julie tries so hard but she _____ in shape.

Must & Can't (for certainty)

We use **must** to say that we are sure that something is true.
Uncle Harry must be fit. He's been jogging for hours!

We use **can't** to say that we are sure that something is not true.
You can't be exhausted. You've been sleeping all morning!

Must and **can't** are followed by the bare infinitive.
You must be tired. You've been working all day.
Alexander can't be hungry. He ate four slices of pizza.

3 Match.

1. Elena's mum is an aerobics teacher.
2. George can't swim yet.
3. Nicholas and Jemma have been studying all morning.
4. Our science teacher is away on holiday.
5. Samantha has always wanted to be on TV.
6. The band's song was awful.

a. They can't be the winners of the song contest!
b. They must be exhausted now.
c. She must be very fit!
d. That can't be her over there!
e. That can't be him in the pool.
f. That must be her on the reality show.

Must

We can also use **must** to talk about obligation and necessity in the present and in the future.
We must always stop at a red light.
I must post the letter tomorrow.

We use **mustn't** to talk about something that we are not allowed to do in the present and in the future.
We mustn't park here.
They mustn't arrive late for the meeting tomorrow.

Must and **mustn't** are followed by the bare infinitive.
I must finish my work tonight.
I mustn't use a pen in the exam.

We can't use **must** for the past. We use **had to**.
I had to complete my assignment last night.

Must isn't usually used in questions. To ask if someone is obliged to do something, we use the question form of **have to**.
Does she have to reply to all these emails?

Have to

We use **have to** in a variety of tenses to talk about an obligation in the present, future and in the past.
We have to look after ourselves.

Have to is followed by the bare infinitive.
Mum has to cook a lot of food for the party.

Need to & Needn't

We use **need to** in a variety of tenses to talk about necessity in the present, future and in the past.
I will need to complete this report.

We use **needn't** to talk about a lack of necessity in the present.
You needn't buy some milk. Dan has already bought some.

Need to and **needn't** are followed by the bare infinitive.
Fred needs to hand in his assignment.
You needn't cook anything as Jenny is taking us out for dinner.

Mustn't vs Don't have to

Mustn't and **don't have to** have a totally different meaning. We use **mustn't** to say that we are not allowed to do something.
We mustn't talk in the library.

We use **don't have to** to say that it isn't necessary to do something, but we can do it if we want to.
You don't have to go swimming if you don't want to.

Mustn't and **don't have to** are followed by the bare infinitive.
You mustn't wake the baby.
You don't have to cook dinner.

4 Complete the sentences with the correct form of **must, mustn't, have to, don't have to** or **needn't** and the verbs in brackets. Sometimes more than one answer is possible.

1 You _don't have to cook/needn't cook_ tonight. I've ordered Chinese. (cook)
2 I _____ eating a hamburger a day! I've got very high cholesterol. (stop)
3 We _____ our dancing lesson. Our teacher gets very angry! (miss)
4 I'm so glad I _____ lunch at school yesterday! The food was awful! (eat)
5 Last year, Dad _____ on a diet. None of his clothes fitted him! (go)
6 I _____ to buy some lettuce for the salad. (forget)

5 Circle the correct words.

Nowadays, we are all very busy and we have very little free time. This is why we (1) must / **have** to eat healthily and exercise whenever we (2) can / could.

We (3) mustn't / needn't eat too many convenience foods and we (4) have to / will be able to make sure we eat a lot of fruit and vegetables.

In the past, we (5) could / can just walk to school or work, but now we drive everywhere so we 6) must / were able to take up a sport. This (7) needn't be / couldn't be a strenuous sport if you don't have very much energy.

We (8) mustn't / don't have get used to a sedentary lifestyle as we'll put on weight.

So, the next time you look in the mirror and say 'Oh! This (9) can't be / must be me, I am so overweight!' think about the advice I have just given you. You (10) could / will be able to notice the difference in no time!

6 Look at the situations and complete the sentences using an appropriate phrase which includes a modal verb.

1. The travel agent said we would stay at a luxury hotel. We have just arrived and we are shocked as there isn't even a toilet in the room!
   This _____*can't be*_____ a luxury hotel.
2. We are on holiday and there's lots of food in the camper van for us to eat.
   We _____ at a restaurant tonight.
3. Last night I made a pizza because I had tomatoes, olives and peppers.
   I _____ a pizza last night.
4. Two teenagers see a young man playing tennis. He is playing very well.
   He _____ a professional tennis player.
5. A lady is looking at her daughter swinging on monkey bars. She remembers doing the same thing when she was a little girl.
   I _____ on monkey bars when I was my daughter's age.
6. A family is at an amusement park. The little girl wants to go on the rollercoaster but she isn't tall enough.
   She _____ the rollercoaster because she isn't tall enough.

7 Complete the second sentence so that it means the same as the first. Use between two and five words.

1. It is necessary that you cut down on chocolate. **to**
   You _____*have to cut down on*_____ chocolate.
2. Nichole has broken her leg so I'm sure she's not at the aerobics class. **can't**
   Nichole has broken her leg so _____ at the aerobics class.
3. When I was younger, I could do the splits. **was**
   When I was younger, I _____ do the splits.
4. Don't do the vacuuming, I've already done it. **needn't**
   You _____ the vacuuming.
5. I'm sure there's an escalator at the shopping mall. **must**
   There _____ at the shopping mall.
6. Dad had a check-up six months ago so he doesn't need to have another one. **have**
   Dad _____ to have another check-up.

Speaking

Imagine you are at summer camp. Talk to your partner about the following things using modals.

- wake up at eight o'clock
- play various sports
- eat everything on our lunch tray
- take part in arts and crafts
- make our beds
- tidy our room
- sweep the floor
- play board games in the evening
- the lights go out at ten o'clock

We have to wake up at eight o'clock.

We can play various sports.

Lesson 2

Modals 2: May, Might, Should & Ought to

May and might

We use **may** and **might** to show possibility.
We *may* eat out tonight.
I *might* go to the concert this weekend.

We use **may** to ask for and to give permission.
May I buy a packet of crisps, Mum?
Yes, you *may* have some ice cream.

May and **might** are followed by the bare infinitive.
Keith *may come* over tonight.
We *might watch* a DVD after dinner.

Remember!
We don't use the question form of *might* and we usually say *might not* instead of *mightn't*.
I don't feel well. I *might not* go to the party.

1 Look at the pictures and complete the sentences with the correct form of **may** or **might** and these verbs.

~~be~~   book   buy   go

1 Thomas ___may/might be___ allergic to nuts.

3 _____ we _____ on a first-aid course?

2 No, you _____ a new toy car.

4 My classmates and I _____ a table at the new restaurant.

73

Should

We use **should**
- to give advice.
  You should eat more healthily.
  You shouldn't play computer games for many hours.
- to ask for advice.
  Should I complain to the manager?
- to make a prediction.
  It's an easy recipe. I should be able to make the casserole.

Should is followed by the bare infinitive.
You should exercise more often.

Ought to

We use **ought to** to give advice.
We all ought to do more exercise.
Dan ought not to eat cheese if he's allergic to it.

Ought to is rarely used in the question form.

Ought to is followed by the bare infinitive.
Brian ought to tidy his room more often.

2 Read the problems and give advice. Use **should**, **shouldn't**, **ought to** or **ought not to** and these verbs. Sometimes more than one answer is possible.

donate   eat   read   sit   take   walk

1 I usually have eggs and bacon for breakfast. I know it's not healthy but breakfast is my favourite meal.
   You _should/ought to eat_ cereal for breakfast.

2 My friends and I are very busy and we don't have time to take up a sport. Our parents drive us to school every morning.
   You and your friends _____ to school.

3 When I get home from school, I'm exhausted. I just want to watch a little TV but when I get up to do my homework, it's time for bed.
   You _____ in front of the TV all afternoon.

4 Mum's in the office all day. She doesn't have time to exercise.
   She _____ the stairs.

5 I always eat health food bars but it seems that they are high in calories, too.
   You _____ the nutritional information on the packet.

6 I've got lots of old clothes and shoes. I don't know what to do with them.
   You _____ your old clothes to charity.

3 Circle the correct words.

1 (May) / Should I come to the art gallery with you, please?
2 We **ought not / shouldn't** to do graffiti in the park.
3 **Ought to / Should** supermarkets and department stores be open on Sundays?
4 **Might / May** I have a bunch of bananas and half a watermelon, please?
5 You really **should / may** recycle batteries, too.
6 Isabel **should / ought** keep the pet tarantula in the garden.

4 Complete the telephone conversation. Use should, ought, may or might.

Alison: Dr Hansen, I've been feeling awful for a couple of days and I think I (1) ___may/might___ have the flu. What (2) _____ I do?

Dr Hansen: Well, the first thing you (3) _____ to check is whether you've got a temperature or not.

Alison: I see. (4) _____ I book an appointment to see you, please?

Dr Hansen: Well, you (5) _____ not get out of bed really, as you (6) _____ get worse.

Alison: OK, well, (7) _____ I take some antibiotics?

Dr Hansen: You don't need antibiotics if it's just a common cold. What you really (8) _____ to do is relax, eat healthily and make sure you drink orange juice. You (9) _____ not feel better immediately, but in a couple of days, you (10) _____ be well enough to go back to work. If you still feel ill in a couple of days, call me and I'll come and see you.

Alison: OK, thank you.

5 Rewrite the sentences using the words given. Use between two and five words.

1. It's possible that Gina has got asthma. **may**
   Gina __________ asthma.
2. It's not a good idea to eat products that contain lots of sugar. **to**
   You _____ eat products that contain gluten.
3. Is it alright if I order dessert? **I**
   _____ order dessert?
4. It isn't a good idea to drink fizzy drinks. **not**
   You _____ drink fizzy drinks.
5. We believe that Ian will pass his final exams. **should**
   Ian _____ exams.
6. I probably won't go to the party tonight. **not**
   I _____ come to the party tonight.

Speaking

Talk with your partner about what advice you would give in these situations using the correct form of may, might, should or ought to.

Situation 1
Paul doesn't like meat but he needs to eat proteins. What should or shouldn't he do?

Situation 2
Brad has put on lots of weight. He has tried dieting but it hasn't worked so far. What ought he to do and what other options might he try?

Situation 3
Maggie wants to take up a sport but she doesn't like strenuous sports. Which sports might she like?

Situation 4
Giselle and Hannah love sweets. They're young but they already have tooth decay. What should they do to stop eating sweets?

Paul should eat fish and nuts.

Brad ought to do more exercise.

6 Lesson 3
Modal Perfect Forms

Modal Perfect Forms

We can use modal verbs with **have** and a past participle to talk about past actions and states.

Possibility

We use **could have + past participle** to talk about something that was possible in the past, but didn't happen.
Why did you eat the whole cake? You could have made yourself sick.

We use **may/might have + past participle** to talk about something that was possible in the past but we don't know whether it happened or not.
Isabel might have wanted to take up a new hobby.
My little brother may have broken the glass.

Certainty

We use **must have been + past participle** when we are sure something was true in the past.
Natalie got 100% for her French exam. She must have studied very hard.

We use **can't/couldn't + past participle** when we are sure that something was not true in the past.
You can't have seen Tom at the sports centre. He's in Germany!
Harry couldn't have made this meal. He can't even boil an egg!

Criticism

We use **shouldn't have/ought not to have + past participle** to talk about something that we disapproved of in the past.
Timothy shouldn't have drunk the whole bottle of lemonade.
You ought not to have been so rude to the salesman.

1 Circle the correct words.

1. You **can't have seen** / must have seen Sally yesterday. She's been in hospital since Friday.
2. David could have helped / can't have helped with the preparations but he didn't.
3. The living room looks great! The children ought not to have tidied / must have tidied it!
4. You really shouldn't have taken / may have taken Katie's ball.
5. George must have won / can't have won the lottery. He's bought a really expensive car.
6. The children might have wanted / ought to have wanted another drink.

2 Look at these situations and complete the sentences using the words given. Use between two and five words.

1 Tommy finished a whole pizza and now he can't move! **should**
   Tommy _____should have eaten_____ less pizza.
2 We had a lot of homework but James said that he finished it all in fifteen minutes. I don't believe him! **have**
   James _____ homework in fifteen minutes.
3 Paul accidentally dropped his father's laptop. He thinks it might be broken. **broken**
   Dad, _____ your laptop. I'm not sure though.
4 My colleagues threw away lots of paper. It's such a waste. **to**
   My colleagues _____ away the paper.
5 It's possible that they bought a house in the countryside. **may**
   They _____ in the countryside.
6 I left my sandwich on the table and when I returned, it had disappeared. My dog was lying on the floor nearby. **must**
   My dog _____ the sandwich.
7 I hadn't studied so I looked at Carrie's answers during the test. Now, we're both in trouble. **have**
   You _____ Carrie's answers during the test.
8 We took the boat to the island and it took ages! It would have been a better idea to fly there. **could**
   You _____ to the island instead.

3 Look at the pictures and complete the sentences with the correct perfect modal form. Use these verbs. Sometimes more than one answer is possible.

| fail | go | make | put | send | solve |

1 Why did you put the baby on the chair?
   He _____could have fallen_____ .

2 My mum _____ the cake while I was at school.

3 The little boy _____ the puzzle.

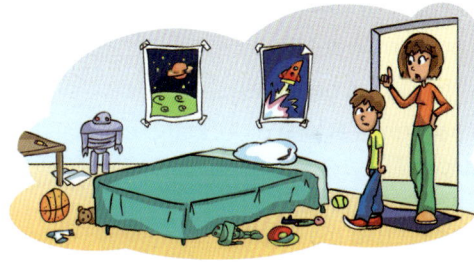

4 You _____ all your toys on the floor!

5 Faye and Mel _____ these flowers for my birthday.

6 Kids, look at the time, you _____ to bed by now.

4 Choose the correct answers.

1 This chicken is tasteless! I _____ to add salt.
   a) may have forgotten
   b should have forgotten
   c ought to have forgotten

2 Sandra _____ started dieting. She looks much slimmer now.
   a can't have
   b ought to have
   c must have

3 There's too much butter in this cake. You _____ to have used my recipe.
   a ought
   b could
   c may

4 We really _____ all those cookies!
   a couldn't have eaten
   b mustn't have eaten
   c shouldn't have eaten

5 Rosemary can't sing very well. She _____ the talent contest.
   a must have won
   b can't have won
   c should have won

6 Peter _____ a car. I don't see him at the bus stop anymore.
   a can't have bought
   b may have bought
   c ought to have bought

5 Complete the dialogue with these words.

can't have digested   could have ended up   may have forgotten
must have eaten   ought to have listened   shouldn't have played

Dora: Are you OK, Max?
Max: I am now, but I (1) _shouldn't have played_ in the volleyball match.
Dora: Why? What happened?
Max: I had lunch at one o'clock and the match was at two. Mum told me not to play, and I (2) _____ to her. During the match, I felt awful. The coach (3) _____ that I had told him I had just eaten and he told me to play.
Dora: Oh dear.
Max: Yes, I (4) _____ lunch too quickly.
Dora: In an hour, you (5) _____ your food, can you?
Max: No, exactly. I (6) _____ in hospital. Now I know next time. No food before a match.

Speaking

Imagine that something has disappeared from your bedroom. Talk with your partner about what disappeared and what may have happened to it. Use the suggestions and the perfect modal form.

- threw it away accidentally
- Mum put it in a drawer
- left it at a friend's house
- sister hid it

I can't have thrown my iPod away accidentally.

Mum may have put my iPod in a drawer.

Units 5 & 6

1 Complete the sentences with the correct form of the Future Simple, **be going to** or the Future Continuous. Use the verbs in brackets.

1 Lizzie promises she ___won't take up___ an extreme sport. (not take up)
2 In a few years, we _____ new sources of energy. (use)
3 Look! Tina is first, she _____ the swimming race. (win)
4 Turn down the volume on your computer or I _____ it _____ . (turn off)
5 What _____ in three hours' time? (you / do)
6 Sam has decided that she _____ as a volunteer this summer. (not work)
7 I can't wait! This time next week, I _____ in the sea. (swim)
8 Mum, _____ me to school tomorrow? (you / drive)

2 Make sentences. Use the Future Perfect Simple or the Future Perfect Continuous.

1 soon / I / pick up / every plastic bottle / on this beach
   ___Soon I will have picked up every plastic bottle on this beach.___
2 ? / the temperature / reach / minus ten / by tonight
   _____
3 Grandma's flight / not land / in ten minutes
   _____
4 I / not get / my driving licence / by the end of the year
   _____
5 on 1st March / we / live / in our flat / for six years
   _____
6 by six o'clock / I tidy / my room / for two hours
   _____

3 Complete the sentences using future tenses. Use the verbs in brackets. Sometimes more than one answer is possible.

1 I bet Dad ___will forget___ to buy me an MP4 player for my birthday. (forget)
2 In two years' time, the biologist _____ his research. (complete)
3 This time next week, we _____ from university! (graduate)
4 Can we go now? In ten minutes, we _____ in this cave for two hours! (hide)
5 Jo has decided she _____ in the competition next week. (not take part)
6 It's too cold to walk to school. I think I _____ the bus. (catch)

4 Circle the correct words.

1 (Would you) / Are you able to lend me your rucksack, please?
2 Unfortunately, we couldn't / won't be able to visit our grandparents at the farm this weekend.
3 I tried very hard, but I can't / wasn't able to finish the crossword.
4 My little sister can't / couldn't ride a horse until she was eleven years old.
5 We can / couldn't take the catamaran or the ferry.
6 Could you / You are able to drive me to the leisure centre, please?

5 Complete the sentences with **can't be** or **must be**.

1 She doesn't speak German. She ___can't be___ a German teacher!
2 Roger has been working on his experiment all day. He _____ tired.
3 Natasha always does well in tests. She _____ a good student.
4 That _____ your mobile phone, it's mine!
5 Eric has gone on holiday for a week. He _____ happy!
6 Nicky hasn't eaten much all day. She _____ on a diet.

79

Review 3

Units 5 & 6

6 Choose the correct answers.

1 I've got a map so we _____ ask for directions.
   a needn't ✓
   b mustn't
   c don't have

2 _____ book a cabin on the cruise ship?
   a Must we
   b We ought to
   c We have to

3 If you don't like fairgrounds, you _____ to come with me.
   a mustn't
   b needn't
   c don't have

4 You were very lucky. You _____ hurt yourself.
   a shouldn't
   b could have
   c could

5 I failed the maths test so I _____ retake it yesterday.
   a must
   b had to
   c must have

6 This water is very dirty, so you _____ drink it.
   a mustn't
   b don't have to
   c needn't

7 John got a bike for his birthday so he _____ walk to school anymore.
   a doesn't have to
   b needs
   c mustn't

8 Jennifer _____ to say she wasn't coming.
   a don't have to call
   b should call
   c ought to have called

7 Complete the text. Use these words. Sometimes more than one answer is possible.

may   may not   might not   ~~must~~   ought   should

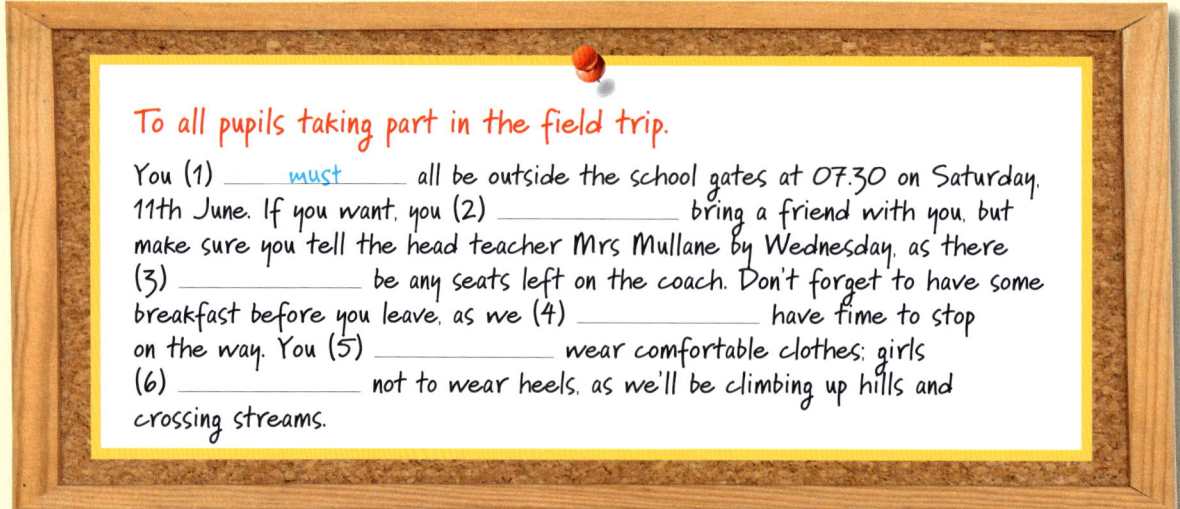

To all pupils taking part in the field trip.

You (1) _must_ all be outside the school gates at 07.30 on Saturday, 11th June. If you want, you (2) _____ bring a friend with you, but make sure you tell the head teacher Mrs Mullane by Wednesday, as there (3) _____ be any seats left on the coach. Don't forget to have some breakfast before you leave, as we (4) _____ have time to stop on the way. You (5) _____ wear comfortable clothes; girls (6) _____ not to wear heels, as we'll be climbing up hills and crossing streams.

80

Writing Project

1 Look at a project about health and fitness. Complete the project with these words.

> can see   have to eat   might be   must be   must have known   need to stop   ought
> should cut down   should eat   will continue   will have crossed   will have finished

A healthy mind in a healthy body

In the ancient world, people (1) _must have known_ what they were talking about when they said 'a healthy mind means a healthy body'.

Nowadays, we all know that the key factors to well-being are a balanced diet and exercise. This doesn't mean that we (2) _____ eating our favourite foods, we just (3) _____ in moderation. We (4) _____ a lot of fruit and vegetables but we (5) _____ on carbohydrates and sugars. As well as a healthy diet, we (6) _____ to make sure that we exercise whenever we have the chance. Walking, jogging, playing a team sport on a regular basis, even everyday household chores are just some of the activities that help us maintain a healthy body.

Many people have started to include physical activities into their leisure time. Take this father and son for instance, we (7) _____ that they are hiking on a mountain. They (8) _____ on a day hike, which means that they (9) _____ the hike by the end of the day and won't stay anywhere overnight. In a moment, the little boy (10) _____ the stream and the two of them (11) _____ their hike. They (12) _____ enjoying themselves as they are spending quality time together.

2 Now it's your turn to do a project about health and fitness. Find or draw a picture of an aspect of health and fitness and write about it.

Lesson 1

Zero Conditional, First Conditional & Second Conditional

Conditional Sentences

Conditional sentences have got two clauses; an *if* clause and a *result* clause. It doesn't matter which clause comes first, but if the *if* clause comes first, we use a comma.
If it's a nice day, we'll go to the beach.
We'll go to the beach *if it's a nice day*.

When we form negative conditional sentences, the negative form can be used in one or both clauses.
If you don't know Cathy's address, I'll tell you.
If James doesn't have breakfast, he won't have energy.

But when we form conditional questions the question form is only used in the result clause.
Will you go to the park if you have time?

Zero Conditional

We use the **zero conditional** to talk about facts and general truths.
If you exercise, you feel good.

We use the **Present Simple** in both the *if* clause and the *result* clause.
If you heat water to 100°C, it boils.

Note that we can use **when** instead of **if** with the zero conditional.
When I don't sleep enough, I get a headache.

1 Complete the sentences with the zero conditional. Use the verbs in brackets.

1 If you ___recycle___ , you ___help___ the planet. (recycle, help)
2 I _____ well in exams when I _____ . (do, revise)
3 If you _____ Russia during winter, the weather _____ very cold. (visit, be)
4 Plants _____ if you _____ them regularly. (grow, water)
5 If we _____ the air-conditioning on all day, it _____ a lot of electricity. (leave, consume)
6 When you _____ the spell check on your computer, you _____ making spelling mistakes. (use, avoid)

The first conditional

We use the **first conditional** to talk about things that are likely to happen in the present or in the future.
If you miss the bus, you'll be late for work.

The *if* clause uses **if** and the **Present Simple**, the **Present Continuous** or the **Present Perfect Continuous** and the *result* clause uses the **Future Simple**.
If I take the bus to work, I will save money on petrol.
If you are looking for Josh, you'll find him in the library.
If they haven't heard the news yet, I'll tell them.

We can use modal verbs like **can, must** and **may** instead of **will**.
If I miss the seven o'clock bus, I may be late.

We can use **unless** with the first conditional to mean **if not**.
If we don't make an effort, we won't find alternative sources of energy.
Unless we make an effort, we won't find alternative sources of energy.

We can also use **provided / providing (that)** and **as long as** with the first conditional.
Providing (that) you don't have any homework, you can go out.
You can go swimming as long as the sea is clean.

We can use imperatives in either clause of a first conditional sentence.
If you've finished, go home.
Finish quickly, and I will let you go home.

2 Write sentences with the first conditional.

1 you / have / more job opportunities / if / you / speak / foreign / languages
   You will have more job opportunities if you speak foreign languages.

2 unless / it / rain / there / be / a drought
   _____

3 as long as / Nicky / try hard / she / succeed
   _____

4 if / I / improve / my general knowledge / I / feel / much happier
   _____

5 Jason / get / the position / providing / he / know / Spanish
   _____

6 we / not / go / on a picnic / unless / it / be / a nice day
   _____

Second Conditional

We use the **second conditional** to
- talk about something that is unlikely to happen in the present or in the future.
  We'd travel the world if we had enough money.
- give advice.
  If I were you, I'd exercise more.
- talk about something which is impossible in the present or in the future.
  If the sun's rays weren't so harmful, I'd sunbathe all day long!

The *if* clause uses **if** and the **Past Simple** and the *result* clause uses **would/could** and the **bare infinitive**.
If we lived in the city centre, we wouldn't need a car.

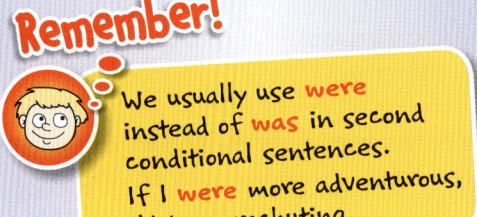

Remember!
We usually use **were** instead of **was** in second conditional sentences.
If I **were** more adventurous, I'd try parachuting.

3 Complete the sentences with the second conditional. Use the verbs in brackets.

1. If we ___didn't use___ our cars so much, we ___would reduce___ pollution. (not use, reduce)
2. I _____ recyclable products if I _____ more time. (collect, have)
3. If we _____ the lights for one hour a day, _____ a difference? (turn off, it / make)
4. Daniel _____ to the sports centre if he _____ in such a remote area. (walk, not live)
5. _____ me with my research if I _____ you? (you / help, pay)
6. We _____ if our neighbours _____ so noisy! (not complain, not be)

4 Choose the correct answers.

1. If the power station emitted less pollution, our town _____ so polluted.
   a. isn't
   b. wouldn't be ✓
   c. won't be

2. Providing we all _____ an effort, we can stop climate change.
   a. would make
   b. will make
   c. make

3. _____ temperature decrease if we stop burning fossil fuels?
   a. Will the Earth's
   b. Would the Earth's
   c. Does the Earth's

4. When we _____ some exercise, we feel really good and we sleep better.
   a. will do
   b. do
   c. would do

5. If you _____ a shower instead of a bath, you save water.
   a. have
   b. would have
   c. has

6. If _____ proper cycling lanes, more people would go cycling.
   a. there were
   b. there would be
   c. there was

5 Complete the text with the zero, first or second conditional. Use the verbs in brackets.

If we (1) ___want___ (want) to achieve something, we do our best to make it happen. So, if we had to stop climate change today, we (2) _____ (spend) all our time looking into renewable sources of energy and how they can be used. Let's take wind power for example. It's not new; people have been using it for many years. Windmills were used and are still used to grind grain or pump water. Nowadays, wind turbines are also used in many places around the world. When the wind turns the blades which are connected to a shaft, it (3) _____ (spin) an electric generator to produce electricity.
One or two wind turbines can't make a difference, though. Unless more companies build wind farms which contain many wind turbines, we (4) _____ (not see) a huge change. Wind farms are a simple solution; providing areas (5) _____ (have) plenty of wind, they can be built almost anywhere. If we build many of these wind farms, we (6) _____ (succeed) in producing enough energy for millions of people around the world.

6 Look at the situations and write conditional sentences. Use the words in bold.

1 You have a lot of homework. You can't go to your friend's house before you finish it. **if**
   If I don't finish my homework, I can't go to my friend's house.

2 Your friend is spending too much money. You advise her not to spend so much. **would**

3 We need to find satellite pictures of the solar system. We have to use the Internet. **unless**

4 You leave ice cream in the sun and it melts. **if**

5 You are invited to a party. You won't go without your best friend. **unless**

6 We use our car every day. The public transport in our area isn't efficient. **was**

Speaking

Talk with your partner about these situations using conditional sentences.

Situation 1:
You heat some ice cubes. They melt.

Situation 2:
Your friend is having problems at school. She doesn't know what to do.

Situation 3:
You are day dreaming about winning a million euros.

Situation 4:
You are taking part in a competition. The winner will receive a prize.

Situation 5:
Imagine you were the mayor or your town. What changes would you introduce?

If you heat ice cubes, they melt.

If I were you, I would talk to my teacher about it.

Lesson 2

Third Conditional, Wish & If only

If only I had taken the car today.

Third Conditional

We use the **third conditional** to talk about something that could have happened in the past, but didn't.
If you had turned on the light, you wouldn't have fallen over.

The *if* clause uses **if** and the **Past Perfect Simple** and the *result* clause uses **would have** and the **past participle**.
If you hadn't thrown away those batteries, we would have recycled them.

See the list of past participles on page 159.

1 Complete the sentences with the third conditional. Use the words in brackets.

1. If you ___hadn't forgotten___ to turn off the water, the bathroom ___wouldn't have flooded___. (not forget, not flood)
2. _____ the experiment if Thomas _____ you? (you / carry out, help)
3. I _____ organic vegetables at the market last week if they _____ so expensive. (buy, not be)
4. My classmates and I _____ in the marathon if we _____ revise for a test. (take part, not have to)
5. Mum _____ her clothes by hand if the washing machine _____ yesterday. (not wash, not break down)
6. _____ more trees if the government _____ them to? (the local council / plant, advise)

86

2 Complete the dialogue with the third conditional. Use the verbs in brackets.

Tom: I can't believe the local community centre has closed down.
Mary: I know. It's terrible, but even if we (1) _____had tried_____ (try), we (2) _____ (not be able) to do anything.
Tom: I don't agree.
Mary: Why, what (3) _____ (you / do) if (4) _____ (you / know) it was going to close down?
Tom: Well, if somebody (5) _____ (tell) us, we (6) _____ (arrange) a gathering at the village square to come up with a plan to stop it from closing.
Mary: Anyway, the problem was the running costs. There wasn't enough money to maintain the centre. The electricity bills were too high. Maybe if we (7) _____ (save) energy, it (8) _____ (make) a difference.
Tom: You see, you agree with me. If the authorities (9) _____ (inform) us, we (10) _____ (raise) money for the centre; bazaars, things like that.
Mary: Mm, you're right.

Wishes (for the present)

We use **wish** or **if only** and the **Past Simple** or the **Past Continuous** when a situation in the present is different to what we would like it to be.
I wish I knew about astronomy. (But I don't know about astronomy.)
If only we didn't live in the city centre. (But we do live in the city centre.)
I wish it wasn't raining. (But it is raining.)
If only I were relaxing by the sea. (But I'm not relaxing by the sea.)

We can't use **if only** in the question form. We must use **wish**.
Do you wish you were a famous singer?

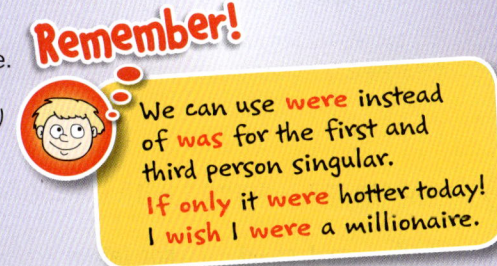

Remember! We can use **were** instead of **was** for the first and third person singular.
If only it were hotter today!
I wish I were a millionaire.

3 Complete the sentences. Use the correct form of these verbs.

| have | know | ~~live~~ | not be | spend | visit |

1 If only I _____lived_____ nearer to my friends in the city centre! The countryside is so boring.
2 The school children wish they _____ more about hydroelectric power.
3 Brad wishes there _____ a nuclear power station in his area.
4 If only my grandson _____ me more often.
5 I wish Dad _____ less time at the office. He's never home!
6 Rosie wishes she _____ a better laptop.

Wishes (for the past)

We use **wish** or **if only** and the **Past Perfect Simple** or the **Past Perfect Continuous** to say that we would like a situation in the past to have been different.
Ivan wishes he hadn't forgotten his keys. (But he did forget them.)
If only they had caught the thief. (But they didn't catch the thief.)
I wish he hadn't been driving so fast. (But he was driving fast.)
If only we hadn't been making a lot of noise. (But we were making a lot of noise.)

4 Look at the situations and complete the sentences using the words in bold.

1. Sam forgot to send me a text message and she feels bad. **forgotten**
   Sam wishes she ___hadn't forgotten to send___ me a text message.
2. I drew graffiti in the school playground and now the head teacher wants to see me. **hadn't**
   If only _____ in the school playground.
3. Celia didn't take responsibility for her actions. **had**
   Celia wishes she _____ for her actions.
4. Mum didn't buy a microwave and now she regrets it. **bought**
   Mum wishes _____ a microwave.
5. I didn't spend very much time on my history project. **spent**
   I wish I _____ on my history project.
6. Katie didn't know how to use a projector and her presentation didn't go well. **known**
   If only Katie _____ how to use a projector.

Wishes + would (for the present and the future)

We use **wish** / **if only** + **would** + **bare infinitive**
- to talk about an annoying action someone does in the present.
  If only you wouldn't make such a mess in my office!
- when we want an action (not a state) to change in the future.
  Dad wishes Mandy and I would watch less television.

Note that we never use **wish** / **if only** + **would** to talk about ourselves.

---

5 Complete the sentences with **I wish**/**if only** and **would**. Use these verbs.

| find   not cheat   not forget   not hide   not stay   tour |

1. ___If only/I wish___ you ___wouldn't forget___ to turn off the lights every night.
2. Daniel _____ his little brother _____ his magazines.
3. Our biology teacher _____ we _____ during tests.
4. _____ our government _____ a solution to the financial crisis.
5. My parents _____ I _____ out late.
6. _____ the famous R & B star _____ Greece.

---

6 Circle the correct words.

1. I wish the visitors don't throw / (wouldn't throw) rubbish on the sand.
2. If only I had won / win first prize for the science project.
3. Sandy wishes she didn't have to use / doesn't have to use so much paper in the office.
4. If only my team had scored / would score a goal in the match yesterday evening.
5. I wish the local council would ban / banned cars from entering the city centre.
6. If only it were / is sunnier in the UK.

88

7 Choose the correct answers.

1 If these trainers _____, everyone would have bought a pair.
   a would catch on
   b had caught on
   c caught on

2 I wish you _____ such a mess in the office every day!
   a don't make
   b hadn't made
   c wouldn't make

3 We _____ if the waves were higher.
   a would go surfing
   b could have surfed
   c will have gone surfing

4 I wish we _____ to go on the school excursion next week.
   a hadn't had
   b didn't have
   c hadn't

5 More people _____ in the fire if the locals hadn't helped people escape.
   a would be injured
   b would have been injured
   c had been injured

6 If only _____ all the firewood!
   a we hadn't used up
   b we wouldn't use up
   c we haven't used up

Speaking

Talk with your partner about how you would like your neighbourhood to be different. Use **I wish** and **if only** and these suggestions to help you.

- more parks
- cleaner
- not so many blocks of flats
- cycling lanes
- sports centre
- cinema complex

Lesson 3

Conditionals with Modal Verbs

Conditionals with modal verbs

We can use **modal verbs** in first, second and third conditional sentences.

In first conditional sentences, we can use **can, could, will, would, should, ought to, might, must** and **needn't** and a **bare infinitive** in the *result* clause.
If we want to be healthy, we must have a balanced diet.

In second conditional sentences, we can use **could, would, should, ought to** and **might** and a **bare infinitive** in the *result* clause.
If we lived closer to our school, we could walk there every morning.

In third conditional sentences, we can use **could, would, should, ought to, might** and **needn't** and a **perfect infinitive (have + past participle)** in the *result* clause.
I might have come to the adventure playground if you had invited me.

Note that we can sometimes use **modal verbs** in the *if* clause.
If he can help, call him.

1 Complete the sentences. Use the first or the second conditional and the words in brackets.

1 The train _ought to arrive_ soon unless there _is_ a delay. (ought to, arrive, be)
2 Jennifer _____ the radio when she _____ to bed. (can, turn off, go)
3 If Harry _____ hard, he _____ the painting today. (might, try, finish)
4 As long as Katrina _____ me to the sports centre in the car this evening, you _____ me there. (needn't, walk, drive)
5 If I _____ on an intensive course, I _____ speak Spanish very soon. (should, go, be able to)
6 Natalie _____ music and films if she _____ a computer. (could, download, have)
7 You _____ the plants providing it _____ . (needn't, water, rain)
8 If we _____ together, we _____ many things! (could, work, achieve)

2 Read the text and then complete the sentences using the modal verb given.

We went to Disneyland last year, but what an experience! Our flight to Paris was delayed and we arrived at our hotel at eleven o'clock. Unfortunately, the hotel restaurant had already closed so we couldn't have dinner. We were very hungry.

The next day, we took the bus to Disneyland. When we arrived at the gate, we couldn't go in straight away because we had forgotten our entry tickets. We had to go back to the hotel to get them! Eventually we got into Disneyland. It was amazing! We spent all day on the rides and we really enjoyed ourselves.

At the end of the day, we decided to buy some souvenirs. But when we went to the counter to pay my purse wasn't in my pocket. Perhaps I had lost it when we were on the rides, so my friend paid for my shopping!

Disneyland was great, but lots of things went wrong!

1 If our flight hadn't been delayed, we _wouldn't have arrived at our hotel at eleven o'clock_. (wouldn't)
2 If we had arrived at the hotel earlier, we _____. (could)
3 If we had remembered our entry tickets, we _____ straight away. (could)
4 If we had remembered our tickets, we _____ to the hotel. (needn't)
5 If I hadn't put my purse in my pocket, I _____ lost it. (might not)
6 My friend _____ if I hadn't lost my purse. (needn't)

3 Complete the sentences with these words.

~~could we have seen~~	might have finished	needn't have bought
ought to have told	shouldn't have come	you could have had

1 _Could we have seen_ the stars if we had looked through the telescope?
2 If _____ any of these iPhones, which one would you have chosen?
3 We _____ our experiment if the bell hadn't rung.
4 If James had known the truth, he _____ me.
5 Anthony _____ to our garden party if he hadn't been feeling well.
6 You _____ a new dishwasher if you'd repaired the old one.

4 Circle the correct words.

1 If you like being outdoors, you **should enjoy** / wouldn't enjoy the National Park.
2 If Marilia hadn't sold her flat in central London, she couldn't have bought / needn't have bought her beautiful cottage.
3 If you want to exercise daily, you should take / needn't take the dog for a walk.
4 Danny needn't study / must study medicine if he doesn't want to become a doctor.
5 Could / Ought to you translate this document for me if I need it for my job?
6 You could have hurt / should have hurt yourself if you'd fallen down that hill.

5 Look at these situations and complete the sentences. Use the words in bold.

1. There may be a storm, so we should stay home. **ought**
   If there is a storm, we _____ought to stay_____ home.
2. It's possible that they can solve the problem. That's why they want to build a dam. **might**
   If they build a dam, they _____ the problem.
3. We don't know enough about alternative sources of energy so we can't use them yet. **could**
   If we knew more about alternative sources of energy, we _____ them.
4. Marcus didn't hear about the protest. It's possible that he wanted to come. **may**
   Marcus _____ to the protest if he had heard about it.
5. It was possible for you to get the job. It wasn't a good idea to insult the IT manager. **might**
   If you hadn't insulted the IT manager, you _____ the job.
6. Penny may teach me how to use the machine. If she does, you don't need to help me. **needn't**
   If Penny teaches me how to use the machine, you _____ help me.

Speaking

Talk with your partner about what advice you would give these people. Use can, could, will, would, should, ought to, might, must and needn't do.

PROBLEM 1
My maths teacher always shouts at me. I'm doing the best I can, but that's not good enough.

PROBLEM 2
My parents are really strict. They don't allow me to go out with my friends.

PROBLEM 3
I only get ten euros pocket money a week. That isn't enough. How can I earn some money?

PROBLEM 4
My next-door neighbour makes a lot of noise all day and even very late at night. What can I do?

If you want to earn some money, you could deliver newspapers.

You should talk to your teacher about it if you believe that you are doing your best.

Lesson 1

Gerunds & Infinitives

Gerunds

Gerunds are nouns. They are formed from verbs with the **–ing** ending.

We use **gerunds**
- as the subject of a sentence.
  Dumping rubbish in the street is a crime.
- as the object of a sentence.
  I love *shopping* with my friends.
- after prepositions.
  My family and I are interested *in diving*.
- after the verb **go** when we talk about activities.
  The twins often *go climbing* at the weekend.
- after certain verbs and phrases:

admit (to)	enjoy	like
avoid	fancy	love
be used to	feel	mention
can't help	hate	miss
can't stand	have difficulty	practise
consider	imagine	regret
deny	it's no use	risk
dislike	it's not worth	spend time
(don't) mind	keep	suggest

I *miss spending* time with my best friend.

Note that certain verbs like **feel, hear, listen to, notice, see** and **watch** are followed by an object pronoun or a noun and then the gerund.
I *felt him looking* at me.

1 Look at the pictures and complete the sentences with gerunds formed from these verbs.

climb   exercise   not recycle   play   sing   walk

1 My cousin and I spend a lot of time ___exercising___ at the weekend.

4 The boys at our school often go _____ at the weekend.

2 _____ in the forest really helps Andrew relax.

5 Penelope is really good at _____ the piano.

3 Natalie regrets _____ her old magazines.

6 My grandfather listens to the birds _____ every morning.

Full Infinitive

We use the **full infinitive** after certain verbs or phrases:

afford	fail	plan
agree	forget	prepare
allow	hope	pretend
appear	invite	promise
arrange	learn	refuse
ask	make an effort	seem
begin	manage	start
choose	need	want
decide	offer	
expect	persuade	

Remember! We use the **bare infinitive** after modal verbs. I **should buy** a new mouse pad.

We *arranged to go* to the beach after school.

We also use the **full infinitive** after certain adjectives: **afraid, angry, anxious, ashamed, glad, happy, kind, nice, pleased, sad, sorry, stupid, surprised, upset, willing.**
I was *surprised to hear* that you lost your mobile phone.

Note that certain verbs like **advise, choose, force, expect, tell** and **persuade** are followed by an object pronoun or a noun and the infinitive.
I *persuaded my brother to lend* me his laptop.

2 Complete the diary entry with full infinitives formed from these verbs.

ask buy buy give give go hear look

Last week it was my birthday and it was one of the best birthdays I've ever had. My godparents usually buy me clothes, but this year they decided (1) __to buy__ me something I wanted. The only thing I really wanted was an iPhone but I was too shy (2) _____ for this. When they offered (3) _____ me money instead, I agreed.

I asked my parents for money, but Dad didn't like this idea and he (4) refused _____ me any. Instead, my parents bought me some books and clothes. I made an effort (5) _____ happy with their presents, but of course I wasn't!

Two days later, to celebrate my birthday, my friends persuaded me (6) _____ to a charity dance. We bought some raffle tickets and danced for most of the night. When the time came to announce the winner of the first prize, I was surprised (7) _____ I had won, as I never win raffles! The prize was a voucher from a huge electrical shop. I couldn't believe it! With this voucher, together with the money my godparents gave me, I could afford (8) _____ the iPhone I wanted!

Gerunds & Infinitives

Some verbs are followed by a **gerund** or a **full infinitive** without a change in meaning:
begin, bother, continue, hate, like, start
My friends and I love communicating on facebook.
My friends and I love to communicate on facebook.

The following verbs are followed by a **gerund** or a **full infinitive** but there is a change in meaning:

forget
Julie forgot telling her mum about the party. (She told her mum about the party but she doesn't remember doing it.)
Julie forgot to tell her mum about the party. (She didn't remember to tell her mum about the party.)

go on
Jennifer went on playing for hours. (She didn't stop playing.)
Jennifer went on to play with her new toy. (She stopped what she was doing and then started to play.)

regret
I regret giving Dennis my old mobile phone. (I wish that I had not given Dennis my old mobile phone.)
I regret to give you some bad news. (I feel sorry that I have to give you some bad news.)

remember
I remember posting the invitations. (I posted the invitations and I remember doing it.)
I remembered to post the invitations. (The invitations have been posted now.)

stop
We stopped eating meat a year ago. (We don't eat meat anymore.)
We stopped to eat a sandwich. (We stopped (working, walking, etc) so that we could eat a sandwich.)

try
Try drinking some milk before you go to bed. (Do this as an experiment because it may help you.)
I know it's difficult, but try to do it. (Make an attempt but it may not be possible.)

3 Circle the correct words.

1 I'm afraid I don't remember to send / **sending** you this email.
2 I don't go shopping / to shop with my mum very often.
3 I've got a really bad headache. Please stop to shout / shouting.
4 My little brother regrets to lock / locking himself in his bedroom.
5 Henry completed a course in computer studies and went on to study / studying at university.
6 Melina, remember to turn off / turning off your computer before you go to bed.
7 The workmen stopped to have / having a break because they were tired.
8 Try to drink / drinking some milk to help you sleep.

4. **Complete the sentences with gerunds or full infinitives. Use the verbs in brackets.**

1. The judge delayed ___announcing___ the winner of the competition last night. (announce)
2. I don't feel like _____ to the beach this afternoon. (go)
3. I told you _____ careful, but you didn't listen to me. (be)
4. I'm sorry _____ that your grandfather is not well. (hear)
5. Robert isn't very good at _____ letters. (write)
6. My friends and I were playing in the park when it began _____ . (rain)
7. Did you notice the little boy _____ on the doorstep? (sit)
8. We regret _____ passengers that the eight o'clock train has been cancelled. (inform)

5. **Complete the second sentences so they have a similar meaning to the first sentences. Use the words in bold.**

1. It's silly to go into town because the shops close in half an hour. **worth**
   It's ___not worth going___ into town because the shops close in half an hour.
2. Nicola tries not to call her friends in Australia because phone calls are very expensive. **avoids**
   Nicola _____ her friends in Australia because phone calls are very expensive.
3. His parents won't let him stay up late. **allow**
   His parents won't _____ late.
4. My family and I are sad that we don't spend weekends in the country anymore. **miss**
   My family and I _____ in the country.
5. James said he'd help us with the shopping. **offered**
   James _____ with the shopping.
6. Polly loves to take photographs of unusual buildings. **taking**
   _____ of unusual buildings is something Polly loves.
7. 'Why don't we go to New York for Christmas?' she said. **suggested**
   She _____ for Christmas.
8. I enjoyed seeing my old students last week. **nice**
   It _____ my old students last week.

Speaking

Talk with your partner about these activities. Use gerunds and infinitives.

I love playing computer games.

I don't enjoy watching football matches.

Lesson 2

Clauses of Purpose

Clauses of Purpose

We use **clauses of purpose** to explain why someone does something or why something happens. We introduce them using these words and phrases:

in order to
We use **in order to** only when the subject of the two clauses is the same. It is followed by the bare infinitive. In negative sentences, we put the word **not** before **to**.
Borrow my memory stick in order to save your data.
I wrote a list in order not to forget anything.

so as to
We use **so as to** only when the subject of the two clauses is the same. It is followed by the bare infinitive. In negative sentences, we put the word **not** before **to**.
My parents go for a walk after dinner so as to get some exercise.
I didn't tell Janet everything so as not to upset her.

in case
We never use **will** or **would** after **in case**, even if we are referring to the future. In this case, we use the **Present Simple**, the **Present Continuous** or the **Present Perfect Simple**. It is followed by a noun or a subject pronoun (I, you, he, etc) and a verb.
I need my cash card in case I run out of money.

so that
We can use **so that** when the object of the two clauses is the same or different. It is followed by a noun or a subject pronoun (I, you, he, etc) and a verb in the **Present Simple** or **can/could** or **will/would**.
John goes jogging every day so that he stays fit.
Lilly has a piggy bank so that she can save money.
We didn't take a break so that we would finish early.

for
We use a noun or an object pronoun after the word **for**.
My mum made some fruit salad just for me.

to
To is followed by the bare infinitive.
We collected money to buy our teacher a present.

1 Circle the correct words.

1 Katie got ready quickly **so that** / for she wouldn't be late.
2 Dee sent us a text message so as / **to** invite us to her party.
3 Take some extra money with you to the mall **in case** / to you see something you like.
4 I'll take the bus home to / **so as not to** walk.
5 I'm leaving the office early today so that / **in order to** buy a new keyboard.
6 We need a table **for** / so that our new printer.
7 Shall we get started, in order to / **so as** not to waste time?
8 I'll finish my homework now for / **in order not to** stay up late.

2 Choose the correct answers.

1 Julian asked me to meet him after school _____ tell me a secret.
   a **in order to**
   b for
   c so as

2 Our teacher explains everything very clearly _____ we don't have any problems.
   a in order
   b so that
   c for

3 The children stopped talking _____ upset their teacher.
   a in order not to
   b in case
   c so as to

4 I need to buy a pump _____ inflate these balloons.
   a for
   b in order
   c to

5 Let's take some money with us _____ we go to the planetarium after school.
   a to
   b for
   c in case

6 I wrote myself a reminder _____ forget my appointment.
   a in case
   b so as not to
   c to

7 Let's buy our tickets online _____ avoid waiting in a queue.
   a so as to
   b for
   c in case

8 Mandy called the bank manager _____ a loan.
   a in order to
   b for
   c so as to

3 Complete the sentences. Use these words.

| for | for | in case | in case | in order not to | so as to | so that | ~~to~~ |

1 Melissa wanted to go to the Internet café _____to_____ meet her friends.
2 Wear your watch during the exam _____ you can check the time.
3 I stopped the celebrity _____ get her autograph.
4 Take some warm clothes with you _____ it snows.
5 We drove to a little restaurant in the country _____ lunch.
6 Julie used a calculator _____ make a mistake.
7 I'll take a hat with me _____ it's sunny.
8 I bought this cool T-shirt just _____ you.

4 Join the sentences. Use the words in brackets.

1. I bought a book about reptiles. I want to learn more about them. (in order)
   I bought a book about reptiles in order to learn more about them.

2. Mum and Dad cycle to work. They want to consume less petrol. (so as to)

3. I left home early. I didn't want to be late. (in order not to)

4. Julian came to my house yesterday evening. We watched the football final together. (so that)

5. My classmates and I are going to the video shop this afternoon. We want to rent a film. (to)

6. Sandra has to go to the electronics shop later on. She needs to fix her GPS. (so as to)

7. I'm taking my headphones to school today. We might have a lesson in the language lab. (in case)

8. Dad bought some beautiful flowers. It's Mum's birthday today. (for)

5 Complete the advertisement. Use only one word in each blank.

LAPTOP AND MOUSE FOR SALE

I'm selling my laptop! It's black and silver and it's only a year old. It comes with a mouse, which is also black and silver, and a black case (1) __to__ help you keep the laptop in good condition.

If you're interested, send me a text message on 6978 840 984 (2) _____ that I can contact you. Unfortunately, you can't see the laptop at the moment, as I've taken it to the local electrical shop (3) _____ a service, but leave me your number in (4) _____ for me to send you a photo.

Just in (5) _____ you're wondering why I want to sell the laptop, I'm selling it so (6) _____ to buy an even newer one!

Speaking

Imagine you are going on a hike in the mountains with your friends. Talk with your partner about what you would take with you and why. Use these ideas to help you.

- compass
- mosquito repellent
- mobile phone
- sunblock
- map
- plenty of water
- first aid kit
- hat
- sandwiches
- whistle

I'd take a hat so as not get sunstroke.

I'd take a whistle in case I got lost.

Lesson 3
Causative

Causative

We use the **causative** to talk about something
- that someone does for us.
  I*'m having* my photos *developed*.
- unpleasant that happened to us that we didn't want to happen.
  Harry *had* his iPad *stolen* last night.

We form the **causative** with the verb **have** + object + past participle of the main verb.
John *has* his clothes *ironed*.

See the list of past participles on page 159.

We can use **by + agent** to show who does the action.
The Adams family had their house redecorated *by an interior designer*.

Note that when we are speaking, we can use the verb **get** instead of **have**. However, when we talk about unpleasant events, we must use **have**.
We*'re getting* a new home cinema *delivered* this evening.
Our neighbours *had* their car *stolen* last week.

Present Simple	I *have* my car *washed*.
Present Continuous	I*'m having* my car *washed*.
Past Simple	I *had* my car *washed*.
Past Continuous	I *was having* my car *washed*.
Present Perfect Simple	I*'ve had* my car *washed*.
Present Perfect Continuous	I*'ve been having* my car *washed*.
Past Perfect Simple	I *had had* my car *washed*.
Past Perfect Continuous	I*'d been having* my car *washed*.
Future Simple	I*'ll have* my car *washed*.
Future Continuous	I*'ll be having* my car *washed*.
Future Perfect Simple	I*'ll have had* my car *washed*.
be going to	I*'m going to have* my car *washed*.
modals (present)	I *must have* my car *washed*.
modals (past)	I *should have had* my car *washed*.

Remember! The object of a causative sentence must appear before the past participle of the main verb. I've had **my computer upgraded**.

1 Complete the sentences with the causative. Use the correct present tense and the words in brackets.

1. I ____am having my new printer delivered____ this afternoon. (my new printer / deliver)
2. Toby's hair grows very fast. He _____ every month. (his hair / cut)
3. Do the children _____? (their rooms / tidy)
4. We _____ now because it's raining. (our windows / not clean)
5. Does Mrs Davies _____ every week? (her house / clean)
6. Next month, we _____ . (our home cinema / fix)
7. They _____ anymore. (the newspaper / not deliver)
8. At the moment, my classmates and I _____ . (our new uniforms / fit)

2 Complete the sentences with the causative. Use the correct past or future tense and these verbs.

| cut | develop | make | not deliver | not publish | paint | ~~steal~~ | water |

1. Last night, my neighbours ____had____ their TV ____stolen____ .
2. We _____ our garden _____ by Stan for years before he retired.
3. The award-winning author _____ her book _____ a week ago.
4. Before the photo studio closed last night, I _____ my photos _____ .
5. This time tomorrow, Julie _____ her hair _____ at the hairdresser's.
6. I _____ my car _____ red before I sold it.
7. The children _____ their new furniture _____ at eleven o'clock this morning.
8. I _____ my curtains _____ by John next week.

3 Read the dialogues and complete the sentences using the causative form.

1. **A:** Oh, your kitchen looks lovely! Did you paint it yourself, Martha?
   B: No, I didn't. I ____had my kitchen/it painted____ by a professional decorator.

2. **A:** Are you going to iron those shirts yourself?
   B: No, I'm not. I _____ by Mum.

3. **A:** Do you go shopping at the supermarket every week?
   B: No, I never go shopping at the supermarket. I go online, place my order and _____ to my home.

4. **A:** Henry's garden is so big. It must take him ages to do the gardening.
   B: He doesn't do it himself. He _____ for him for years.

5. **A:** Is Jennifer making your wedding cake for you?
   B: No, she isn't. We _____ by the Delicious Cake Company.

6. **A:** Has your computer been repaired now?
   B: Yes, but it cost a lot of money. I _____ before I realised that the local shop could have done it more cheaply.

4 Rewrite the sentences using the words given. Use between two and five words.

1 Toby often washes Veronica's car. **has**
Veronica ___often has her car washed___ by Toby.

2 Our general manager has arranged for her office to be furnished next week. **having**
Our general manager _____ next week.

3 The technician has set up a wireless Internet connection. **had**
We _____ wireless Internet connection set up.

4 I must arrange for the rubbish to be collected. **have**
I _____ collected.

5 Helen is going to arrange for somebody to build her a new cupboard. **built**
Helen is going to _____ .

6 A gardener planted some flowers for me yesterday. **planted**
I _____ by a gardener yesterday.

7 A cleaner was cleaning my house all day yesterday. **cleaned**
I _____ all day yesterday.

8 Cathy should have arranged for somebody to water the garden. **had**
Cathy _____ .

9 A famous fashion designer will design a dress for Gabriella. **will**
Gabriella _____ by a famous fashion designer.

10 Tommy was in pain after the dentist pulled out his tooth. **had**
Tommy _____ out by the dentist.

Speaking

Talk with your partner about what Nellie is dreaming. Use these ideas and the causative.

- do homework / teacher
- tidy room / brother
- walk my dog / sister
- carry my school bag / friend
- wash my hair / hairdresser
- make meals / famous chef

I'm having my homework done by my teacher.

I'm having my room tidied by my brother.

Review 4

Units 7 & 8

1 Complete the sentences. Use the words in brackets.

1 If you ___press___ this button, the computer will turn off. (press)
2 Dan _____ his cash card unless he runs out of money. (not use)
3 _____ slippery if it rains? (this road / be)
4 If I cycled to school, it _____ me fifteen minutes. (take)
5 _____ if you kept it away from the sunlight? (this plant / grow)
6 We _____ late if we hadn't missed the bus. (not arrive)

2 Look at these situations and write conditional sentences.

1 Jeremy dropped his monitor and it broke. He needed to buy a new one.
   If Jeremy hadn't dropped/broken his monitor, he wouldn't have needed to buy a new one.
2 The sink is full of dishes but I don't have time to wash them.
   _____
   _____
3 Your friend has asked you for some advice. Her parents are upset with her because she lied to them. You think she should apologise.
   _____
   _____
4 Robbie and his mum are shopping. He wants a new computer game but his mum doesn't buy it for him because she thinks it's very expensive.
   _____
   _____
5 Judy left her keys at her friend's house. She couldn't open her front door.
   _____
   _____
6 A teacher is telling her students that they'll go on an excursion providing their test results are good.
   _____
   _____

3 Circle the correct words.

1 It's very hot today! I wish I (had brought)/ brought some sun cream with me.
2 The train ride last night was so boring. If only I took / had taken my MP4 player with me.
3 I'm trying to sleep and the dogs are making a noise. I wish they would stop / had stopped barking.
4 Colette won second prize in the diving competition. She wishes she came / had come first.
5 This dress costs €150! I wish it weren't / isn't so expensive.
6 I'm expecting a call for a new job. If only the phone would ring / had rung!

4 Choose the correct answers.

1 If the fire brigade had arrived earlier, the building _____ .
   a wouldn't burn down
   (b) wouldn't have burnt down
   c would burn down
2 Unless we service the air-conditioning unit, we _____ .
   a hadn't turned it on
   b didn't turn it on
   c shouldn't turn it on
3 If I _____ where your memory stick was, I would tell you.
   a know
   b had known
   c knew
4 As long as your brother _____ with you, you can go to the party.
   a goes
   b will go
   c went
5 What a noise! I wish you _____ your electric guitar in the middle of the night.
   a hadn't played
   b don't play
   c wouldn't play

103

Review 4

Units 7 & 8

5 Complete the text with gerunds or full infinitives. Use the verbs in brackets.

A month ago, our school decided (1) _to take part_ (take part) in a competition. The aim was for students from all the schools in our area to prepare a presentation called *The future of our environment through the eyes of the youth of today*.

My three classmates and I agreed (2) _____ (prepare) a presentation and for two weeks, we spent time (3) _____ (look) for information and photos on the Internet.

When the day of the competition arrived, we all gathered at the school. My classmates and I weren't willing (4) _____ (go) first, so we watched the others. Their presentations were so professional, like something Dad would prepare. Our turn came and even though I can't stand (5) _____ (speak) in front of an audience, I did. Our presentation wasn't as amazing as the others, but we managed (6) _____ (express) our opinion and we felt happy.

My classmates and I were very surprised (7) _____ (hear) that we had won. Even though my friends told me not to, I couldn't help (8) _____ (ask) the judges how they had come to their final decision. 'It was easy,' the judge told me. 'It was obvious you had spent time (9) _____ (prepare) your presentation and you managed (10) _____ (get) your points across very well, so well done!'

6 Join the sentences. Use the words in bold.

1 Mark is going to study medicine. He wants to become a doctor. **in order to**
   Mark is going to study medicine in order to become a doctor.

2 Don't hang out the washing. It might rain. **in case**
   _____

3 Helen turned on the heating. She felt cold. **so as not to**
   _____

4 The museum is closed to visitors. It is being renovated. **for**
   _____

5 Susie picked up the watering can. She wanted to water the plants. **to**
   _____

6 I'm saving my pocket money. I want to buy a new computer. **in order to**
   _____

7 Complete the sentences with the causative. Use the words in brackets.

1 At the moment, I _am having my digital camera repaired_ . (digital camera / repair)
2 My family and I usually _____ once a week. (house / clean)
3 In a couple of hours, the singer _____ . (her song / not record)
4 _____ we _____ tomorrow? (our teeth / clean)
5 I believe the school _____ very soon. (new library / build)
6 Our head teacher _____ this afternoon. (a solar panel / install)
7 Theresa always _____ to her house on Friday evening. (pizza / deliver)
8 Mum _____ last week. (the ironing / not do)
9 David _____ for him before he learnt how to cook. (his meals / cook)
10 _____ you _____ when you lived at home? (your clothes / iron)

104

Writing Project

1 Look at a project about an environmentally-friendly structure. Choose the correct words.

If you (1) **take / took** a walk around London, you'll see this very impressive and unusual architectural structure. It's London's first environmentally friendly skyscraper. It is called the 'Swiss Re Tower' as the Swiss Reinsurance Company (2) **had it constructed / had constructed it**.

It is 180 metres tall and there are 40 floors. It is also known as 'The Gherkin' because it looks like a gherkin. The building is covered in glass, (3) **in order to / for** allow natural light and ventilation, (4) **so that / so as to** energy consumption can be reduced. In summer, warm air is removed from the building and in winter, solar heating is used to warm the building. Moreover, natural light passes through the building (5) **so that / for** a more pleasant working environment. At the same time, the cost of lighting is very low. In fact, if we (6) **compare / compared** its consumption to that of a regular building, we'd see that it is actually 50% less.

The Swiss Re Tower is certainly out of the ordinary, but it is surprising (7) **to hear / hearing** that many Londoners wish such a building (8) **hadn't been built / wasn't built** in the centre of the City Of London.

2 Now it's your turn to do a project about an environmentally-friendly structure. Find or draw a picture of the building and write about it.

Lesson 1

Reported Speech: Statements

Reported Speech

We use **reported speech** to tell someone what another person has said.

When we report something, we change the tense to a tense further back in the past as follows:

Direct Speech
Present Simple
'Ella works in tourism,' Tom said.
Present Continuous
'Ella is working in tourism,' Tom said.
Present Perfect Simple
'Ella has worked in tourism,' Tom said.
Present Perfect Continuous
'Ella has been working in tourism,' Tom said.
Past Simple
'Ella worked in tourism,' Tom said.
Past Continuous
'Ella was working in tourism,' Tom said.
Future Simple (will)
'Ella will work in tourism,' Tom said.
Be going to
'Ella is going to work in tourism,' Tom said.
can
'Ella can work in tourism,' Tom said.
must
'Ella must work every day,' Tom said.
may
'Ella may work in tourism,' Tom said.

Reported Speech
Past Simple
Tom said (that) Ella worked in tourism.
Past Continuous
Tom said (that) Ella was working in tourism.
Past Perfect Simple
Tom said (that) Ella had worked in tourism.
Past Perfect Continuous
Tom said (that) Ella had been working in tourism.
Past Perfect Simple
Tom said (that) Ella had worked in tourism.
Past Perfect Continuous
Tom said (that) Ella had been working in tourism.
would
Tom said (that) Ella would work in tourism.
Was going to
Tom said (that) Ella was going to work in tourism.
could
Tom said (that) Ella could work in tourism.
had to
Tom said (that) Ella had to work every day.
might
Tom said (that) Ella might work in tourism.

Reported Speech

In **reported speech**, we also change personal pronouns (I, you, he, she, it, we, you, they), possessive adjectives (my, your, his, her, its, our, your, their), possessive pronouns (mine, yours, his, hers, ours, yours, theirs) and object pronouns (me, you, him, her, it, us, you, them).

'I found my keys,' Alice said.
Alice said she had found her keys.
'Melanie made me a chocolate milkshake,' Michael said.
Michael said Melanie had made him a chocolate milkshake.

We can use the word **that** after **he/she**, etc **said** and **he/she**, etc **told me/them**, etc.
'I've been sending emails,' she said.
She said (that) she had been sending emails.

Note that we do not need to change tenses when we are talking about something that is still true.
'Harriet is being very supportive,' Julie said.
Julie said that Harriet is being very supportive.

There is also no tense change when the reporting verb is in the present. We also don't change the tense when we are talking about a law of science and with the following: **Past Perfect Simple, Past Perfect Continuous**, second and third conditional sentences, **would, could, might, should, ought to, used to, had better, mustn't** and **must** when it is used to express deduction.

'Eating too many sweets is bad for our health,' says Mum.
Mum says eating too many sweets is bad for our health.
'The sun rises in the east,' said Mr White.
Mr White said (that) the sun rises in the east.
'You should retrain as a teacher,' Mum told Dad.
Mum told Dad that he should retrain as a teacher.

Remember!
When we use **tell** with reported speech it is followed by an object whereas **say** is not followed by an object.
John **told me** (that) Nicky was doing a writing course.
John **said** (that) Nicky was doing a writing course.

1 Complete the sentences in reported speech.

1 'We spent a lot of time in Morocco,' Monica said.
   Monica said _____(that) they had spent_____ a lot of time in Morocco.

2 'Our department isn't going to hire any more people,' the manager said.
   The manager said _____ any more people.

3 'I've decided to do a teacher-training course,' Jennifer said.
   Jennifer said _____ a teacher-training course.

4 'The jacket may not be leather,' Dad said.
   Dad said _____ leather.

5 'Serena wants to start job hunting,' Chris said.
   Chris said _____ job hunting.

6 'I'll email the applicant,' the secretary told me.
   The secretary told me _____ the applicant.

7 'We were waiting for the courier,' Mum and Dad said.
   Mum and Dad said _____ for the courier.

8 'John handed in his assignment on time,' said Mr Brown.
   Mr Brown said _____ his assignment on time.

2 Complete the dialogues using reported speech. Use the words in brackets.

1 **Vicky:** I'm getting ready for my graduation ceremony. (a party)
  Ross: Oh. I thought you said _you were getting ready for a party_.

2 **Harriet:** Lucy's been working in an estate agency for ten years. (five years)
  Lee: Oh. I thought she said _____.

3 **Miss Clarkson:** I'll get us both some coffee. (tea)
  Clare: Oh. I thought you said _____.

4 **Alice:** David applied for a university grant. (a small business grant)
  Gina: Oh. I thought he said _____.

5 **Dan:** Jane and Tim were working in a factory when it closed down. (museum)
  Joe: Oh. I thought they said _____.

6 **Felicity:** I always send my reports on Thursdays. (Tuesdays)
  Henry: Oh. I thought you said _____.

7 **Duncan:** Kevin can't find Mr Smith's office. (Mrs Smith's office)
  James: Oh. I thought he said _____.

8 **Penny:** You must get your application in by the 15th March. (15th April)
  Liam: Oh. I thought you said _____.

3 Rewrite the sentences in direct speech.

1 Robbie said that he'd been speaking to an economist all morning.
  'I've been speaking to an economist all morning,' Robbie said.

2 My parents told me that I shouldn't come home later than midnight.
  _____ my parents told me.

3 Oliver said that he had never been to a planetarium before.
  _____ Oliver said.

4 Tina said that she was going to be made redundant.
  _____ Tina said.

5 Elizabeth said that she works long hours.
  _____ Elizabeth said.

6 Tamara said that she was working on a company project.
  _____ Tamara said.

Changes in Time and Place

When we use **reported speech**, besides the changes in tenses, personal and possessive pronouns, there are other changes which need to be made to words and phrases that talk about time and place.

today	that day
tonight	that night
tomorrow	the following day/the next day
yesterday	the day before/the previous day
last year	the year before/the previous year
next week	the week after/the following week
a month ago	the month before/the previous month
now	then
ago	before
at the moment	at that moment
here	there
this/these	that/those

'I got a bonus yesterday,' Tim said.
Tim said that he had got a bonus the day before.

'The graduate is being interviewed at the moment,' Celia said.
Celia said that the graduate was being interviewed at that moment.

4 Circle the correct words.

1. Our headteacher said that we had to look smart for the graduation ceremony tomorrow / **the following** day.
2. The applicant said that she had trained to be a chef the year before / last year.
3. Frank told his wife that he would be home early that / this evening.
4. Three days ago, the singer said he was going to sign some autographs for his fans tomorrow / the following morning.
5. Last week, Catherine said that she had worked overtime yesterday / the day before.
6. Mum told us that we had to economise this / that summer.
7. You said that you had put the money here / there.
8. Last Saturday Richard told us that he would visit us tonight / that night.

5 Rewrite the sentences in reported speech.

1. 'I'm going for a job interview tomorrow,' Mandy said.
   Mandy said that she was going for a job interview the next day / the following day.
2. 'We walked around Central Park last week,' Keeley told me.
3. 'The technician is fixing my laptop at the moment,' Luke said.
4. 'My colleagues are going to go out to dinner tonight,' Lynne said.
5. 'We're flying to the States next month,' my boss said.
6. 'There was a huge recession last year,' the accountant said.
7. 'I'm sure I put my keys here,' Mum said.
8. 'Lisa didn't make this mess on the floor,' said Tina.

Speaking

Look at these messages and tell you partner what these people said.

Lesson 2

Reported Speech: Questions, Commands & Requests

Reported Questions

We usually use the verb **ask** to report questions. We often use an object with **ask**.
'Can I have an apple?' Jodie *asked me*.
Jodie *asked me* if/whether she could have an apple.

Questions with Question Words

We use the same **question word** that is in the **direct question**.

Remember! The changes that apply to *reported statements* also apply to *reported questions*.

Direct Speech

Present Simple
'*Whose is* this bag?' he asked.

Present Continuous
'*What is* the boy *drawing*?' asked Mrs Jones.

Present Perfect Simple
'*Who has* the teacher *chosen*?' she asked.

Present Perfect Continuous
'*Who has been making* so much noise?' Jo asked.

Past Simple
'*Where did* you *find* that ring?' she asked.

Past Continuous
'*Why was* the baby *crying*?' Dad asked.

will
'*When will* you *go* to the bank?' Mum asked.

can
'*How* high *can* you *jump*?' Mr Lee asked.

must
'*Which* cough syrup *must* I *take*?' Dad asked.

Reported Speech

Past Simple
He asked *whose* that bag *was*.

Past Continuous
Mrs Jones asked *what* the boy *was drawing*.

Past Perfect Simple
She asked *who* the teacher *had chosen*.

Past Perfect Continuous
Jo asked *who had been making* so much noise.

Past Perfect Simple
She asked *where* I *had found* that ring.

Past Perfect Continuous
Dad asked *why* the baby *had been crying*.

would
Mum asked *when* I *would go* to the bank.

could
Mr Lee asked me *how* high I *could jump*.

had to
Dad asked *which* cough syrup he *had to take*.

1 Look at the pictures and complete the reported questions.

1 The teacher asked
   who was going to tell her the answer.

2 The manager asked
   _____.

3 The employee asked
   _____.

4 The passenger asked
   _____.

5 The boy asked
   _____.

6 Harry asked his brother
   _____.

Questions without Question Words

When a **direct question** doesn't start with **a question word**, we form the **reported question** with the word **if**. We can also use **whether**.

Direct Speech	Reported Speech
Present Simple 'Do you like peanut butter?' Tim asked.	**Past Simple** Tim asked if/whether I liked peanut butter.
Present Continuous 'Are they playing together?' he asked.	**Past Continuous** He asked if/whether they were playing together.
Past Simple 'Did you have lunch?' she asked.	**Past Perfect Simple** She asked if/whether I had had lunch.
Past Continuous 'Were you playing with Ted?' she asked.	**Past Perfect Continuous** She asked if/whether I had been playing with Ted.
Present Perfect Simple 'Have they finished?' she asked.	**Past Perfect Simple** She asked if/whether they had finished.
Present Perfect Continuous 'Have you been exercising?' he asked.	**Past Perfect Continuous** He asked if/whether we had been exercising.
will 'Will you answer the phone, please?' Mum asked. 'Are you going to help me George?' I said.	**would** Mum asked if/whether I would answer the phone. I asked if/whether George was going to help me.
can 'Can I bring a friend to the party?' the man asked.	**could** The man asked if/whether he could bring a friend to the party.
must 'Must I drink all the milk?' Kelly asked.	**had to** Kelly asked if/whether she had to drink all the milk.

---

2 Circle the correct words.

1 Sandra asked **if I lived** / did I live in the city centre.
2 My brother asked me whether I had eaten / did I eat a whole pizza the night before.
3 The receptionist asked were we going to check out / if we were going to check out that morning.
4 Angela asked the history teacher does she have to / whether she had to learn the text off by heart.
5 William asked me if I was studying / have I been studying botany for long.
6 Tony asked whether if he could write / he could write about wildlife for his school project.
7 The teacher asked us if we had finished / whether we have finished the test.
8 Mum asked me if I liked / do I like her new dress.

3 Read the job interview and complete the sentences using reported speech. Only report the words in bold.

Mr Oliver: Good morning Josh, my name is Mr Oliver. I'm the Human Resources Manager.
Josh: Good morning, Mr Oliver.
Mr Oliver: Josh, **why do you want to work in the film industry?**
Josh: Because my degree is in media studies and it's my dream to be a film producer.
Mr Oliver: I see. **What work experience do you have?**
Josh: **I've been working for a local production company for six years.**
Mr Oliver: **Why did you decide to look for another job?**
Josh: **I want to advance my career,** to work in a larger company.
Mr Oliver: I see. Now, **do you speak any foreign languages?**
Josh: Yes, I speak French and Spanish.
Mr Oliver: And **when can you start working for us?**
Josh: **I need to give my current boss a month's notice.** Then, I can start.
Mr Oliver: Thank you Josh. **I'll contact you at the beginning of next week.**
Josh: Thank you Mr Oliver. **I'll be expecting your call.**

1 Mr Oliver asked Josh <u>why he wanted to work in the film industry</u>.
2 Mr Oliver asked Josh _____.
3 Josh said (that) _____.
4 Mr Oliver asked Josh _____.
5 Josh said (that) _____.
6 Mr Oliver asked Josh _____.
7 Mr Oliver asked Josh _____.
8 Josh said (that) _____.
9 Mr Oliver said (that) _____.
10 Josh said (that) _____.

Commands

Reported commands are usually introduced with the verb **tell**. **Tell** is followed by an object and the full infinitive. When the command is negative, we put **not** before the full infinitive.

'*Post* these letters as soon as possible,' my supervisor said.
My supervisor *told me to post* those letters as soon as possible.
'*Don't spend* all your money,' Dad said.
Dad *told me not to spend* all my money.

Requests

Reported requests are usually introduced with the verb **ask**. **Ask** is followed by an object and the full infinitive. When the request is negative, we put **not** before the full infinitive. Note that we leave out the word **please** in reported requests.

'Please *come* along to the meeting,' Rosanne said.
Rosanne *asked me to come* along to the meeting.
'Please, *don't make* a lot of noise,' the teacher said.
The teacher *asked us not to make* a lot of noise.

Remember! The changes that apply to reported statements also apply to reported commands and reported requests.

3 Write what the people said in reported speech.

Find out if there are any vacancies in the fast food restaurant.

1 John told me _to find out if there were_ any vacancies in the fast food restaurant.

Make an appointment with the careers advisor.

2 Aunt Helen told Ron _____ an appointment with the careers advisor.

Please make an effort to do well in the test.

3 Mum asked me _____ to do well in the test.

Postpone the match until tomorrow.

4 Our coach told us _____ .

Don't mention the price of this present to Mum.

5 My brother told me _____ .

Please don't forget to call the estate agency.

6 The boss asked his secretary _____ .

Please don't turn on the fax machine.

7 Mrs Wallace asked the secretary _____ .

Don't call me by my nickname.

8 Joe told his parents _____ .

5 Choose the correct answers.

1 Ben asked me whether _____ to school that morning.
   a) I could drive him
   b to drive him
   c please drive him

2 I asked my swimming instructor _____ last year's record.
   a if it had broken
   b who had broken
   c to have broken

3 Elena told me _____ an application letter to the advertising company.
   a whether to not send
   b don't send
   c not to send

4 My manager asked me _____ the presentation by the following week.
   a to finish
   b if I can finish
   c finish

5 Hannah asked her husband _____ so many insects in the kitchen.
   a why there were
   b if there are
   c why were there

6 Eliza asked _____ our homework the following morning.
   a to hand in
   b whether we had to hand in
   c do we have to hand in

7 The twins asked their parents _____ their room that morning.
   a if they had to tidy
   b whether they have to tidy
   c do we have to tidy

8 The policeman told the cyclist _____ in the cycling lane.
   a stay
   b don't stay
   c to stay

Speaking

Imagine that you went for an interview for a summer job teaching English and you got the job. Talk with your partner about what questions the interviewer asked you and what he told you to do and not to do when teaching. Use these ideas to help you.

- Why are you interested in the job?
- Do you have any hobbies?
- How long can you work for?
- Where do you live?
- Do you enjoy working with children?
- Have you ever taught English before?
- Do you speak any foreign languages?
- Can you tell me how you would teach grammar, please?
- Can you explain how you would deal with difficult students, please?
- Tell students to ask questions if they don't understand.
- Tell students to revise vocabulary every day.
- Don't let students eat during the lesson.
- Don't allow students to hand in their work late.

The head teacher asked me why I was interested in the job.

He asked me if I had any hobbies.

Lesson 3

Reporting Verbs

Reporting Verbs

The most common reporting verbs are **say** and **tell** for statements, **tell** for commands and **ask** for questions and requests. However, there are other reporting verbs that we can use to report what a person said more accurately.

Verb + full infinitive

agree	'Yes, I'll come with you,' he said.	He agreed to come with me.
offer	'Shall I get you a drink?' he asked.	He offered to get me a drink.
promise	'I promise I won't be late,' he said.	He promised not to be late.
refuse	'No, I won't give you the ball,' he said.	He refused to give me the ball.
threaten	'Stop fighting or I'll punish you,' he said.	He threatened to punish me if I didn't stop fighting.

Verb + object + full infinitive

advise	'You should eat more fruit,' he said.	He advised me to eat more fruit.
ask	'Could you answer the phone?' he said.	He asked me to answer the phone.
beg	'Please, please tell me,' he said.	He begged me to tell him.
command	'Stand to attention,' he said.	He commanded them to stand to attention.
invite	'Will you come over for dinner?' he said.	He invited me to come over for dinner.
order	'Go to the head teacher's office,' he said.	He ordered me to go to the head teacher's office.
persuade	'Can you clean my room for me, please?' he said.	He persuaded me to clean his room.
remind	'Don't forget to take some money,' he said.	He reminded me to take some money.
warn	'Don't stand near the edge,' he said.	He warned me not to stand near the edge.

Reporting Verbs

Verb (+ preposition) + gerund

admit (to)	'Yes, I broke the glass,' he said.	He admitted (to) breaking the glass.
accuse (sb of)	'You took my pen,' he said.	He accused me of taking his pen.
apologise for	'I'm sorry I didn't tell you the truth,' he said.	He apologised for not telling me the truth.
boast about	'I've got a faster car than you,' he said.	He boasted about having a faster car than me.
complain (to sb of)	'I am taken for granted,' he said.	He complained of being taken for granted.
deny	'I didn't damage your bike,' he said.	He denied damaging my bike.
insist on	'You must go with me,' he said.	He insisted on me going with him.
suggest	'Let's have a break,' he said.	He suggested having a break.

Verbs + that

announce	'I'm going backpacking', he said.	He announced that he was going backpacking.
complain	'You are always late,' he said.	He complained that I was always late.
deny	'I didn't scratch the CD,' he said.	He denied that he had scratched the CD.
exclaim/remark	'What a beautiful painting,' he said.	He exclaimed/remarked that it was a beautiful painting.
explain	'I took the pen by mistake,' he said.	He explained that he had taken the pen by mistake.
promise	'I promise I'll be good,' he said.	He promised that he would be good.
suggest	'You ought to get some rest,' he said.	He suggested that I (should) get some rest.

1 Complete the sentences. Use these words.

> accuse   apologise   boast   complain   explain   offer   refuse   warn

1. 'I got 100% for the French test,' said Carrie
   Carrie ___boasted___ about getting 100% for the French test.
2. 'Don't be late for work again,' my supervisor said.
   My supervisor _____ me not to be late for work again.
3. 'John, you broke the photocopying machine!' said the secretary.
   The secretary _____ John of breaking the photocopying machine.
4. 'I'll drive you to the theatre,' said Mum.
   Mum _____ to drive me to the theatre.
5. 'I'm sorry I broke the mirror,' said the removal man.
   The removal man _____ for breaking the mirror.
6. 'You never want to go anywhere,' my sister said.
   My sister _____ that I never wanted to go anywhere.
7. 'No, I don't want to wear this hat,' said Wendy.
   Wendy _____ to wear that hat.
8. 'I thought Kate wanted me to tell the teacher,' said Jake.
   Jake _____ that he had thought Kate had wanted him to tell the teacher.

2 Circle the correct words.

1. My sister agreed (to help) / helping me with my project.
2. Cathy begged not to tell / me not to tell her secret.
3. Peter denied that he had lost / to loose the keys.
4. Mel suggested having / to have a swim.
5. I promise that I'm not / not to be impolite again.
6. Jack invited us to come / that we come to his party.

3 Complete the sentences in reported speech.

1 'Don't forget to wear a suit for the interview,' Hannah said to her sister.
Hannah reminded her sister _____to wear a suit_____ for the interview.

2 'I didn't leave all these plates in the sink,' Julie said.
Julie denied _____ in the sink.

3 'I'll buy you some new summer clothes,' Mum said to me.
Mum promised _____ some new summer clothes.

4 'Let's call an electrician to install these new light bulbs,' Anna told her Dad.
Anna suggested _____ those new light bulbs.

5 'Put the phone down or I'll call the boss,' Mark said.
Mark threatened _____ if I didn't put the phone down.

6 'I'm sorry, but I won't change my mind,' Jake said.
Jake refused _____ his mind.

7 'You ought to put away your things,' my sister said.
My sister suggested _____ my things.

8 'You must have a hair cut,' said Dad.
Dad insisted _____ a hair cut.

4 Rewrite the sentences in bold in reported speech. Use these verbs.

| advise | agree | apologise | ~~ask~~ | exclaim | insist on | invite | warn |

Last week my kitchen suddenly flooded. I called the plumber but he was busy. I called again and said **'Please come to my house today, it's urgent'**.

The plumber said 'OK, **I'll be there soon,**' and he arrived a couple of hours later. Unfortunately he wasn't able to fix the tap. He said to me **'You shouldn't touch the tap until it's fixed**. I'll come back tomorrow.

As I couldn't cook anything, I decided to order pizza. I didn't want to eat alone so I called my friend and said **'Come and have lunch at my house** today'. A little later, after we had eaten, my friend wanted a glass of water. I said to her **'Don't touch the tap,** the plumber is coming to fix it tomorrow'. She didn't pay attention and she turned on the tap. Suddenly, there was a loud noise and the pipes burst. I looked at her in shock. She said to me **'I'm sorry I didn't listen to you'.** I didn't know what to do, there was water everywhere. She said to me **'I must help you clean up'** so we got a couple of mops and got to work. I was so upset and I said **'What a disastrous day!'**.

1 I asked the plumber/him to come to my house.
2 _____
3 _____
4 _____
5 _____
6 _____
7 _____
8 _____

5 Rewrite the sentences using the reporting verbs in bold.

1 'I'm going to hand in my resignation,' my colleague said. **announce**
   My colleague announced that he was going to hand in his resignation.

2 'There isn't any air conditioning in this building,' the employees said. **complain**

3 'We won't leave until the film finishes,' Tara said. **insist**

4 'What a boring job!' Josh said. **remark**

5 'You have to finish your CV before you start applying for jobs,' my uncle said. **explained**

6 'Put the bag down,' the police officer said to the thief. **ordered**

7 'What a tasty hamburger,' said Johnny. **exclaim**

8 'Please, please help me,' the little boy said to the lady. **beg**

Speaking

Look at the pictures and what the people are saying. Then report what they said to your partner using the reporting verbs given.

1 I'm sorry I deleted your email. **apologise**
2 Don't forget to look at my presentation. **remind**
3 I got a huge bonus! **announce**
4 Don't miss another history lesson. **warn**
5 I'll lend you my iPod at the weekend. **promise**
6 I didn't take your mouse pad. **deny**
7 I'll drive you to school. **offer**
8 It's so cold in here. **complain that**

My sister offered to drive me to school.
He apologised for deleting my email.

Lesson 1
Passive Voice: Present, Past & Future

Passive Voice: Present, Past & Future
We use the **passive voice** when
- we want to emphasise the action rather than who does it.
  A new aquarium *is being built* in the city centre.
- when we don't know who does the action.
  The jewellery *was stolen* from the safe.
- when it's obvious who does the action.
  Many people *were helped* out of the burning building. (by the firemen)

We form the **passive voice** with the auxiliary verb **be** in the same tense as the main verb in the active sentence and the past participle of the main verb. The object of the active sentence becomes the subject of the passive sentence. We use **by** if we want to say who or what (**the agent**) does the action.
My friends *gave* me a lot of presents for my birthday. (active sentence)
I *was given* a lot of presents *by* my friends for my birthday. (passive sentence)

See the list of past participles on page 159.

The verb **let** is used in active sentences, but the verb **allow** is used in passive sentences.
They *let* us take pictures of the aircraft. (active sentence)
We *were allowed* to take pictures of the aircraft. (passive sentence)

Note that we don't use the passive voice in the Present Perfect Continuous, the Past Perfect Continuous, the Future Continuous or the Future Perfect Continuous.

Tense	Active Voice	Passive Voice
Present Simple	She *makes* a phone call.	A phone call *is made*.
Present Continuous	She *is making* a phone call.	A phone call *is being made*.
Present Perfect Simple	She *has made* a phone call.	A phone call *has been made*.
Past Simple	She *made* a phone call.	A phone call *was made*.
Past Continuous	She *was making* a phone call.	A phone call *was being made*.
Past Perfect Simple	She *had made* a phone call.	A phone call *had been made*.
Future Simple	She *will make* a phone call.	A phone call *will be made*.
Future Perfect Simple	She *will have made* a phone call.	A phone call *will have been made*.
be going to	She *is going to make* a phone call.	A phone call *is going to be made*.

1 Complete the sentences with the Simple Present passive, the Present Continuous passive or the Present Perfect Simple passive. Use the words in brackets.

1 When there is an emergency, a lifeguard _____is called_____ (call).
2 Unfortunately, people _____ when an earthquake strikes. (often injure)
3 Mr Steven _____ so we can't start the meeting. (delay)
4 My car _____ at the moment. (not service)
5 Our new furniture _____ yet. (not delivered)
6 Security checks _____ at the airport. (frequently carry out)
7 Houses in the countryside _____ . (often not break into)
8 The school children _____ from the building right now. (rescue)

2 Complete the text with the Past Simple passive, the Past Continuous passive or the Past Perfect Simple passive. Use the verbs in brackets.

The volcanic eruptions in Iceland

Although the Eyjafjallajökull volcanic eruption in spring 2010 was quite small, severe problems (1) _____were caused_____ (cause) in Iceland and all around Europe. In the areas near the eruption, farmers and their families (2) _____ (evacuate) and flights to and from Iceland (3) _____ (postpone).
Seismic activity in the area (4) _____ (detect) towards the end of 2009 before a small eruption occurred in mid March 2010. While this eruption wasn't particularly large, in April 2010 an ash cloud (5) _____ (create). This time, it wasn't just flights to and from Iceland that (6) _____ (affect). In actual fact, flights all around Europe (7) _____ (cancel) for a number of days. By mid May the situation had improved and the volcano (8) _____ (consider) dormant once again.

3 Rewrite the sentences with the Future Simple passive, the passive of **be going to** or the Future Perfect Simple passive.

1 The painter will paint my uncle's house next week.
   My uncle's house will be painted (by the painter) next week.
2 The gardener is going to plant some new flowers.
   _____
3 The dentist will have taken out your tooth by tomorrow.
   _____
4 They aren't going to exhibit the Monet paintings in Rome.
   _____
5 Will the chef have cooked all the food by tonight?
   _____
6 The cleaners won't have cleaned the building by tomorrow morning.
   _____
7 Will he publish his new book this year?
   _____
8 They won't deliver Mum's new car tomorrow.
   _____

4 Look at the pictures and complete the sentences. Use the correct form of the passive and these verbs.

| break into | cut down | extinguish | ~~find~~ | need | present |

1 Hopefully, the shipwreck in the Caribbean Sea ____will be found____ soon.

2 The fire _____ at the moment.

3 Volunteers _____ to help clean up the beaches.

4 Every day, far too many trees _____ in the rainforests.

5 While I was paying for my shopping, my car _____ .

6 Last night, the lifeguard _____ with an award for his bravery.

5 Complete the questions with the correct form of the passive voice using the words in brackets. Then complete the short answers.

1 ____Was the local IT firm purchased____ last week? (the local IT firm / purchase)
Yes, ____it was____ .

2 _____ every afternoon? (tea / serve)
No, _____ .

3 _____ when I visited last night? (twins / feed)
Yes, _____ .

4 _____ at the moment? (the restaurant / renovate)
No, _____ .

5 _____ in the school magazine last week? (my article / publish)
Yes, _____ .

6 _____ tomorrow evening? (the TV / deliver)
No, _____ .

7 _____ a grant? (you / ever give)
Yes, _____ .

8 _____ by the time the guests arrive? (all the food / cook)
Yes, _____ .

6 Complete the second sentences so that they have a similar meaning to the first sentences. Use the words in bold.

1. The government's decision has affected everyone. **been**
   Everyone _has been affected_ by the government's decision.
2. Many people use the tram every day. **used**
   The tram _____ every day.
3. Thousands of spectators watched the World Cup final. **by**
   The World Cup final _____ thousands of spectators.
4. The TV channel broadcast the Eurovision song contest last night. **was**
   The Eurovision song contest _____ last night.
5. The local council will open the castle soon. **be**
   The castle _____ by the local council soon.
6. They are going to give my favourite actor a role in the new blockbuster film. **going**
   My favourite actor _____ a role in the new blockbuster film.
7. John and Cathy were sealing the invitations for hours. **sealed**
   The invitations _____ John and Cathy for hours.
8. I have a lot of work to do before I can go out. **must**
   My work _____ I can go out.

7 Complete the article with the correct form of the active or passive voice. Use the verbs in brackets.

Médecins Sans Frontières

Médecins Sans Frontières is an organisation that (1) _is known_ (know) for the medical assistance it (2) _____ (offer) to third world countries and to those that (3) _____ (involve) in war.

Médecins Sans Frontières (4) _____ (establish) in 1971 by a few French doctors, who (5) _____ (believe) that everyone should be able to receive medical care. For about forty years now, health care and medical training (6) _____ (give) to people in many different countries thanks to this organisation.

The organisation (7) _____ (refer) to as Médecins Sans Frontières worldwide, but English-speaking countries often use the name 'Doctors Without Borders'. There are five operational centres, which (8) _____ (locate) in Amsterdam, Barcelona, Brussels, Geneva and Paris. Since the creation of Médecins Sans Frontières, private contributors (9) _____ (provide) most of the organisation's funding. The organisation (10) _____ (present) with the Nobel Peace Prize in 1999 for the work it does.

Speaking

Imagine that you are arranging for help to be sent to a country which has been hit by an earthquake. Talk with your partner about what has been done and what will be done. Use the passive voice and these ideas to help you.

- food / deliver
- clothes / gather
- money / collect
- medical personnel / fly out
- medicines / send
- inhabitants / evacuate
- homes / provide
- rescue workers / call
- fresh water / distribute

Lots of food has been delivered to the people.

Medical personnel will be flown out.

Lesson 2
Passive Voice: Gerunds, Infinitives & Modals

Passive Voice

The **passive voice** can be used with **gerunds, infinitives** and with **modal** verbs.

Tense	Active Voice	Passive Voice
infinitive	She needs to make a phone call.	A phone call needs to be made.
gerund	She likes people calling her.	She likes being called.
modals (present)	She may make a phone call.	A phone call may be made.
modals (past)	She may have made a phone call.	A phone call may have been made.

Note that when the verb **make** means **force**, it is followed by the bare infinitive in the active voice, but in the passive voice it is followed by the full infinitive.
I make my daughter set the alarm every morning.
My daughter is made to set the alarm every morning.

However, when verbs of perception such as **hear** and **see** are used in passive sentences, they can be followed by a gerund or the full infinitive.
I heard the children playing with the ball.
The children were heard playing with the ball.
I saw the man take the money.
The man was seen to take the money.

1 Circle the correct words.

1. The ironing needs **to be done** / do.
2. The letter shouldn't be opened / open.
3. We were made to stay / stay behind.
4. All the children wanted to be chosen / choosing.
5. The boy was seen to break / breaking the window.
6. An exception may have been made / may be made now.

2 Choose the correct answers.

1. An aircraft _____ above the island.
   a. seen to fly
   b. was seen flying
   c. be flying

2. Living conditions in the area should _____ .
   a. be improved
   b. being improved
   c. to be improved

3. The window _____ last night.
   a. was heard to break
   b. is broken
   c. was heard to breaking

4. Overalls ought to _____ by all factory employees from now on.
   a. wear
   b. be worn
   c. have been worn

5. Luke dislikes _____ by his surname.
   a. be called
   b. to be called
   c. being called

6. A state of emergency must _____ immediately.
   a. be declared
   b. being declared
   c. declared

7. You were very lucky. You could _____ very badly.
   a. be hurt
   b. being hurt
   c. have been hurt

8. Nobody wants _____ .
   a. to be taken advantage of
   b. being taken advantage of
   c. to have taken advantage of

3 Complete the sentences in the passive voice. Use the words in bold.

1. Nicky hopes they choose her for the lead role. **be**
   Nicky hopes ___to be chosen___ for the lead role.
2. I can't believe the traffic warden gave me a fine. **given**
   I was surprised _____ a fine by the traffic warden.
3. The lifeguard saw the little girl crying for help. **was**
   The little girl _____ for help by the lifeguard.
4. The firefighters made us leave the forest. **to**
   We _____ the forest by the firefighters.
5. Tod wishes they hadn't chosen him for the main role in the play. **for**
   Tod regrets _____ the main role in the play.
6. I won't let them punish me for something I didn't do. **punished**
   I refuse _____ for something I didn't do.
7. Our teacher doesn't allow us to use calculators during the maths lesson. **not**
   We _____ calculators during the maths lesson.
8. Children love it when their parents take them to the park. **to**
   Children love _____ the park by their parents.

4 Complete the sentences with the passive voice. Use these verbs.

clean   hire   ignore   pay   photograph   repair   take   win

1 Your mortgage must _____be paid_____ soon.
2 Jonathon hates _____ by people.
3 Our dining room table needs _____ by a carpenter.
4 The 2010 Australian Tennis Open should _____ by Andy Murray.
5 We were made _____ up the mess.
6 The chef considered _____ on a part time basis.
7 All the actors wanted _____ on the red carpet.
8 Most children enjoy _____ to the zoo.

5 Write sentences. Use the correct form of the passive voice.

1 Tom / dislike / tell off
   Tom dislikes being told off.
2 the dog / must / feed / twice a day
   _____
3 ? / Jessica / look forward / make / a supervisor
   _____
4 my sister and I / like / invite / to parties
   _____
5 ? / you / appreciate / tell / the truth
   _____
6 you / could / drive / to the party / last night
   _____
7 I / make / tidy / my bedroom / every Saturday
   _____
8 they / not want / left behind / last night
   _____

Speaking

Imagine that your head teacher wants to make some changes at school and has asked for your suggestions. Talk with your partner about what you would suggest using the passive voice and these phrases to help you.

- bigger playground / create
- science lab / build
- whiteboards / install
- other languages / introduce
- school / renovate
- food / improve
- sports facilities / construct
- more teachers / hire

In my opinion, a bigger playground should be created.

I think a science lab must be built.

Lesson 3

Linking Words: Even though, Although, Despite, In spite of, However & Whereas

Linking Words: Even though, Although, Despite, In spite of, However & Whereas
The following **linking words** and phrases can be used to introduce an idea that is the opposite of or contrasts with another idea.

Even though and **although** are followed by a subject and verb.
Even though/Although we played surprisingly well, we lost the match.

Despite and **in spite of** are followed by a noun, a pronoun or a gerund.
Despite/In spite of the risk, Joe jumped into the sea to save the little girl.
Despite/In spite of his wealth, he was very mean.
Despite/In spite of being off duty, the policeman helped us chase the thieves.

Note that we can use **the fact (that)** + subject and verb after **despite** and **in spite of**.
Despite/In spite of the fact (that) there was an emergency exit, it was blocked!

When **even though, although, despite** and **in spite of** come at the beginning of the sentence, we use a comma to separate the two clauses. But when they come in the middle of a sentence between two clauses to show the contrast between them, we don't use a comma.
Despite doing my best, I didn't manage to finish on time.
I didn't manage to finish on time *despite* doing my best.

However and **whereas** are also used to add a comment which contrasts with what has just been said.
However is followed by a comma but we put a comma before **whereas**.
Kim is a great nurse. *However,* she can't stand the sight of blood!
I like to go out, *whereas* my sister prefers to stay home.

1 Circle the correct words.

1 Whereas / **Even though** they are rivals on the football pitch, they are best friends at school.
2 However / Even though there are more policemen patrolling the streets, crime is on the increase.
3 The hooligan was convicted. Whereas / However, he wasn't sent to prison.
4 The police said that nobody was hurt in the riot, whereas / despite I heard that three supporters were sent to hospital.
5 In spite of / Although the road being blocked, Tara got to her interview on time.
6 We got to the station early. However / Although, we still managed to miss the train.
7 Although / However many people came to the party, a lot of food was left over.
8 We went to the beach even though / in spite of the fact that the weather was bad.
9 Despite / Although the evidence, Paul Jones was found innocent.
10 Tom wants to be a policeman when he grows up, in spite of / whereas Jane wants to be a firefighter.

2 Match.

1 Despite the hurricane,
2 There was a hit and run incident in the town centre.
3 I still speak to Jack
4 Although the earthquake didn't last for long,
5 In spite of being environmentally friendly,
6 Jodie is constantly on a diet
7 Despite the problems they have,
8 My sister loves chocolate ice cream,

a despite the fact that she is slim.
b even though he lied to me.
c they are very optimistic about the future.
d However, nobody was seriously injured.
e the death toll was surprisingly high.
f the inhabitants weren't evacuated.
g whereas I love vanilla.
h George never recycles anything.

3 Complete the text with these words.

although   despite   even though   however   in spite   whereas

Dealing with shoplifting

Shop owners all around the world lose a lot of money on a daily basis, as shoplifters have become experts. (1) _Although_ preventing shoplifting is almost impossible, there are a few things that shop owners can do. Shop owners should make sure that there are surveillance cameras in their shops. (2) _____ thieves know that if they are caught, they will be arrested, it's a good idea to remind them; shop owners could put a sign on the shop window 'SHOPLIFTERS WILL BE PROSECUTED'. This may not discourage all of them. (3) _____, it will stop a few. Of course staff shouldn't look at customers suspiciously, (4) _____ they have to be alert and ready to call the police if they notice something strange happening. (5) _____ being criminals, shoplifters aren't stupid and they know their rights, so be careful. (6) _____ of the fact that they are the ones committing the crime, you don't want to be the one arrested for assaulting them.

4 Join the sentences. Use the words in bold.

1. Freddy jumped over the fence. He didn't hurt himself. **in spite of**
   In spite of jumping over the fence, Freddy didn't hurt himself.
2. Maria is a great tennis player. She wasn't voted player of the year at her tennis club. **even though**
3. Danielle is a great volleyball player. She wasn't chosen for the team. **being**
4. Thousands of fans turned up to the cup final. There weren't any hooligans. **however**
5. Rosie lives in a beautiful neighbourhood. There's graffiti everywhere. **although**
6. Vandals broke into my car last night. It was parked opposite a police station. **despite the fact that**
7. John accused me of stealing his calculator. I believe he lost it. **whereas**
8. My parents are quite open-minded. They don't want me to become an actor. **although**

Speaking

Look at the newspaper headlines and talk with your partner about the situations using linking words.

Floods hit region – no casualties!

Economic crisis – thousands of iPads bought every day!!

Riot expected in central London – protest went well!

Bomb scare – Metro not closed!

Thieves caught red-handed – weren't prosecuted!

Scandal revealed – Prime Minister re-elected!

Girl suspected of arson – no evidence!

ADVERSE WEATHER CONDITIONS – MATCH TO GO AHEAD!

Despite the floods, there were no casualties in the region.

Even though the police expected a riot in central London, the protest went surprisingly well.

Review 5

Units 9 & 10

1 Complete the sentences with direct or reported speech.

1 'I'm starting my French course tomorrow,' Kelly said.
Kelly said <u>(that) she was starting her French course the following/next day</u>.

2 The maths teacher told Billy to stop talking.
_____ the maths teacher told Billy.

3 'There was a huge riot in the centre of London last week,' Dad said.
Dad said _____.

4 'Please can you water the plants for me tonight?' Aunt Poppy asked me.
Aunt Poppy asked me _____.

5 'Where is the cinema complex?' my brother asked.
My brother asked _____.

6 'Were you revising all night long?' Tony asked his sister.
Tony asked his sister _____.

7 'You will receive a full grant,' the university lecturer told me.
The university lecturer told me _____.

8 'Could you send a fax for me, please?' my boss asked.
My boss asked _____.

9 Mum told me not to go out in the storm that night.
_____ Mum told me.

10 'The employees must have a lunch break,' the manager said.
The manager said _____.

11 'We watched a DVD before dinner,' the children said.
The children said _____.

12 'Why did you lie to your brother?' Dad asked me.
Dad asked me _____.

2 Choose the correct answers.

1 Jeremy offered _____ to the station.
 a driving me
 (b) to drive me
 c drive me

2 The doctor advised _____ less meat.
 a Mum to eat
 b Mum eats
 c that Mum ate

3 My best friend announced _____ the lottery.
 a has won
 b she wins
 c that she won

4 Harry apologised for _____ my favourite CD.
 a damaging
 b he damaged
 c has damaged

5 Natasha promised _____ her grandparents.
 a visiting
 b to visit
 c visit

6 My dad reminded _____ my keys.
 a taking
 b to take
 c me to take

129

Units 9 & 10

3 Circle the correct words.

On Tuesday, 12 January, 2010 Haiti (1) struck / (was struck) by a huge earthquake that measured 7 on the Richter scale. It was a disaster and hundreds of thousands of people (2) lost / were lost their lives. The Red Cross calculated that nearly one-third of the country's entire population (3) were being affected / had been affected by the quake.

The Haitian Government estimated that 250,000 homes and 30,000 commercial buildings had collapsed or (4) damaged / had been severely damaged. This meant that communication systems (5) broke down / were broken down, many roads (6) blocked / were blocked and many hospitals (7) were destroyed / destroyed, which made the situation even worse.

The world didn't hesitate to act. Aid (8) received / was received from many different countries, a variety of fund raising activities (9) set up / were set up worldwide and money and goods (10) are donated / were donated by countless individuals.

4 Write sentences in the passive voice.

1 Judy loves her dad driving her to school.
   Judy loves being driven to school by her dad.

2 All candidates must fill in this information.
   _____

3 They won't renovate the town hall this summer.
   _____

4 The bricklayer was mixing the cement at seven o'clock this morning.
   _____

5 I've already walked the dogs.
   _____

6 My parents are going to buy a summer house.
   _____

5 Complete the article with these words.

| although | despite | however | ~~in spite~~ | though | whereas |

Chocolate tasting – a delicious job?

Did you know that some people taste chocolate for a living? (1) ___In spite___ of sounding like the best job in the world, chocolate tasting is not always easy.

So, what do chocolate tasters do? To begin with, they do a lot of market research and hold tasting sessions to determine what appeals to consumers. (2) _____ the research, the taster still needs to actually try samples of chocolate. Even (3) _____ there is no set time when chocolates are sampled, most of the tasting is done early in the morning. The tester needs to be slightly hungry and to be far away from anything else with strong tastes or smells.

You may think that tasters sample lots of chocolates in one day. (4) _____, they can only test up to six different chocolates at a time. Successful chocolate tasters can understand what 'good' chocolate is.

(5) _____ they train themselves to predict which chocolates will be successful, they sometimes make mistakes and as a result some of the chocolates chosen aren't a hit with consumers.

Most people believe the chocolate tasters are only interested in the taste of the chocolate, (6) _____ they also pay attention to the way it looks, feels and smells during the tasting session.

130

Writing Project

1 Look at a project about a mountain rescue service. Choose the correct answers.

Mountain rescue

Mountain rescue is a tremendously important service. Its goal is to enable the safe return of people who (1) _____ or have got lost while exploring a mountainous environment. Rescue is usually very difficult and can even be dangerous for the rescue team. Helicopters (2) _____ to rescue people and search dogs may be used to locate injured or lost people.

This photo shows a rescue at the Denali National Park, where many rescues (3) _____ . The national park (4) _____ in Alaska, and it boasts Denali, the highest mountain in North America. Many visitors flock to the national park, which (5) _____ in 1917, for mountain expeditions. (6) _____ climbers are well aware of the dangers they face, many accidents occur as some climbers aren't prepared for the adverse weather conditions they will encounter. (7) _____ of being warned before they set off, they (8) _____ to depend on rescue services for a safe return.

1 a injured   b have been injured   c are injuring
2 a are often used   b often used   c used
3 a are carried out   b carry out   c carried out
4 a locates   b are located   c is located
5 a established   b is established   c was established
6 a Although   b Despite   c In spite of
7 a In spite   b Even though   c Despite
8 a are forced often b are often forced   c are often being forced

2 Now it's your turn to do a project about a rescue service. Find or draw a picture of the rescue service and write about it.

131

Lesson 1
Adjectives & Comparison of Adjectives

Adjectives

When we use two or more adjectives to describe a noun, we usually place the adjectives in the following order:

opinion	size	age	shape	colour	origin	material	noun
beautiful				green		silk	scarf
expensive		new			Italian		suit
	huge		ancient			marble	statue

We can use adjectives after verbs like **appear, be, become, feel, get, look, make, seem, smell, sound, taste** and **turn**. Sometimes we put an adverb between the verb and the adjective.
That dress *looks amazing* on you!
I *feel very hot* in this sweater.

1 Put the words in the correct order to make sentences.

1 silk / bought / expensive / Rebecca / an / scarf / red
   Rebecca bought an expensive red silk scarf.

2 white / the / was / girl / a / straw / wearing / huge / hat
   _____

3 black / suits / prefers / linen / model / the / stylish
   _____

4 Persian / beautiful / rug / a / old / my parents / have got
   _____

5 that / round / don't like / table / is / huge / wooden / that / I
   _____

6 little / drives / amazing / French / Grandpa / an / car
   _____

Comparison of Adjectives

We use the **comparative** form of adjectives to compare two people, animals or things. We often use the word **than** after the **comparative**.
Heidi is older than her brother.
Your skirt is longer than mine.

We use the **superlative** form of adjectives to compare a person, animal or thing with other people, animals or things. We use the word **the** before the **superlative**.
This is the most expensive pair of shoes I've ever bought!
She's the most stylish of all the mothers.

These adjectives have irregular comparative and superlative forms:

Adjective	Comparative	Superlative
good	better	the best
bad	worse	the worst
much	more	the most
many	more	the most
little	less	the least
far	further / farther than	the furthest / farthest

2 Complete the sentences with the comparative or superlative. Use the adjectives in brackets.

1. This is ___the most wonderful___ festival in the country. (wonderful)
2. Catherine's cowboy boots were _____ mine. (expensive)
3. The new boutique in the town centre sells _____ clothes on the market. (trendy)
4. Max is _____ student in my class. (good)
5. Penny is much _____ her sister. (glamorous)
6. Your ball gown is _____ Susie's. (long)
7. Henrietta is wearing _____ diamond I've ever seen! (big)
8. Today's weather forecast is _____ yesterday's. (bad)

(not) as ... as

We can also use **as + adjective + as** to compare two people, animals or things.
We use **as ... as** when the two people, animals or things are the same.
Rebecca is as talented as her father.

We use **not as ... as** when the two people, animals or things are not the same.
This costume isn't as impressive as the first one.

3 Complete the sentences so they have a similar meaning to the first sentences. Use **as ... as** and **not as ... as**.

1. The weather is very nice today. The weather wasn't so nice yesterday.
   The weather yesterday ___wasn't as nice as___ it is today.
2. My dad's watch is expensive. My mum's watch is also expensive.
   My dad's watch _____ my mum's watch.
3. I like hamburgers but they aren't very healthy. Salads are very healthy.
   Hamburgers _____ salads.
4. Mrs Hamilton is a fashionable woman. Her daughter is also fashionable.
   Mrs Hamilton _____ her daughter.
5. Nicholas can run very far because he is really fit. Jemima can only run a hundred metres.
   Jemina _____ Nicholas.
6. I washed my bike today. My brother hasn't washed his bike for a month.
   My brother's bike _____ my bike.

> **the + comparative …, the + comparative …**
> We can use **the** + comparative …, **the** + comparative … to show that something depends on or is influenced by something else. It shows cause and effect.
> *The older* he gets, *the more handsome* he becomes.
> *The more* Judy goes out, *the happier* she feels.

4 Look at these situations and write sentences using **the** + comparative …, **the** + comparative … .

1 Emily is training very hard. She is becoming better at playing tennis.
   The harder Emily trains, the better she becomes at playing tennis.

2 I've been eating more fruit and vegetables. I've started to feel better.

3 Our teacher is giving us more homework. We are complaining more.

4 Jerry has been working overtime. He's feeling tired.

5 We are going to more concerts these days. We are spending more money.

6 I like easy puzzles. They are very enjoyable.

7 John and James have been studying very hard. Their marks are getting better.

8 You aren't being very friendly these days. Your friend is getting upset.

5 Choose the correct answers.

1 The more healthily you eat, the _____ to lose weight.
   a) more likely you are
   b) you are more likely
   c) you are the most likely

2 My new skirt is _____ as Martha's vintage one.
   a more original
   b not as original
   c the most original

3 This is _____ maths exercise I've ever done!
   a more complicated than
   b more complicated
   c the most complicated

4 Celia has been looking for a(n) _____ necklace.
   a unusual pearl white
   b white pearl unusual
   c unusual white pearl

5 _____ people buy designer clothes nowadays than in the past.
   a The fewer
   b Fewer
   c The fewest

6 Frankie isn't _____ as you think.
   a the most old-fashioned
   b as old-fashioned
   c more old-fashioned

7 Jodie's parents gave her a _____ puppy.
   a gorgeous black tiny
   b gorgeous tiny black
   c black gorgeous tiny

8 I think watching DVDs _____ as going to the cinema.
   a is enjoyable as
   b is more enjoyable
   c is as enjoyable

6 **Circle the correct words.**

Billabong clothing, which is one of (1) more popular / **the most popular** brands amongst teenagers today, was founded in 1973. It offers a wide variety of clothing and sportswear and although the items may be slightly (2) more expensive / the most expensive than other brands of clothing, they are (3) the most fashionable / as fashionable as on the market and are becoming even (4) as popular as / more popular with teenagers. These clothes may (5) not be as economical as / be the most economical non-brand clothes but they are very unique. However, the more teenagers wear these brands, (6) the less unique / the more unique they become.

The company also sells Element clothing, items which are just (7) as trendy as / the trendiest Billabong and are very popular with skateboard enthusiasts. So, if you're keen on (8) cool long multicoloured / multicoloured long cool swimming trunks, try Billabong!

7 **Complete the second sentences so they have a similar meaning to the first sentences. Use the words in bold.**

1 Veronica is the rudest person I've ever met. **as**
   I've never met anybody _____*as rude as*_____ Veronica.

2 When it gets hot, it's easy for me to dive into the pool. **easier**
   The hotter it gets, _____ for me to dive into the pool.

3 Henrietta's clothes are more old-fashioned than her sister's. **trendy**
   Henrietta's clothes _____ her sister's.

4 I've never seen such an amazing coat. **most**
   This is _____ I've ever seen.

5 Felicity is more successful than Natasha. **not**
   Natasha is _____ Felicity.

6 Expensive clothing is usually of better quality. **better**
   Usually, the more expensive clothing is, _____ it is.

7 It takes one hour to fly to Athens. It takes five hours to drive there. **is**
   Flying to Athens _____ driving there.

8 I think running is tiring. I think swimming is tiring too. **as**
   I think running _____ swimming.

Speaking

Look at these pictures with your partner. Describe and compare these mobile phones. Use the suggestions to help you.

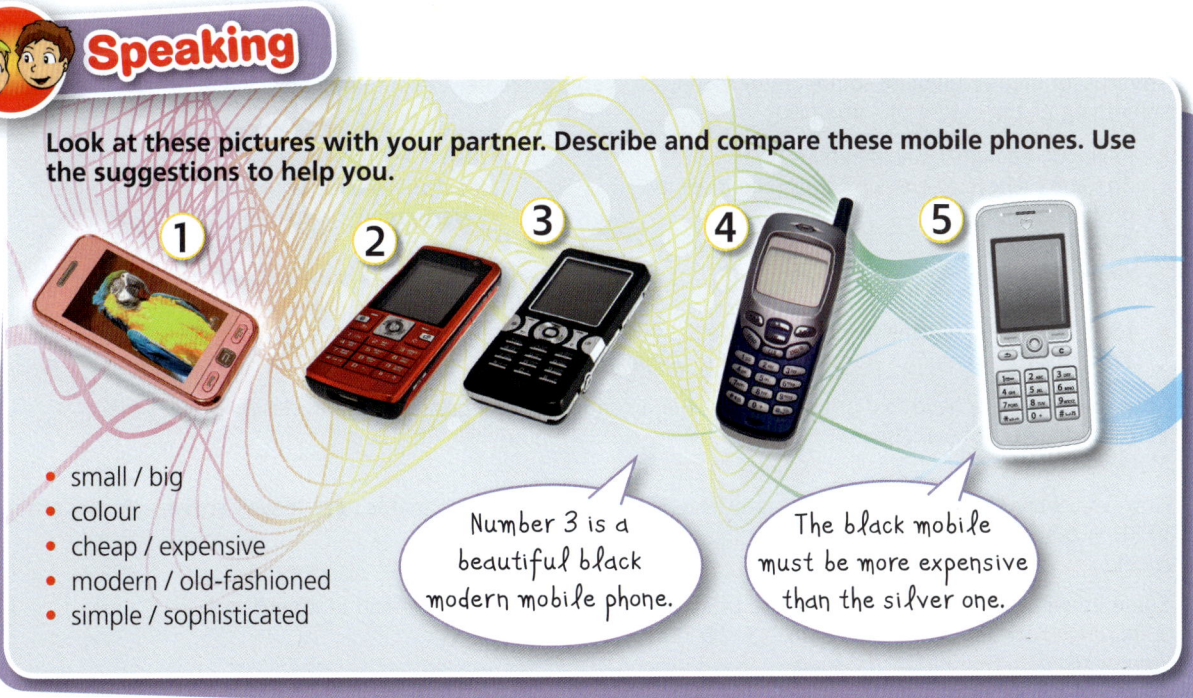

- small / big
- colour
- cheap / expensive
- modern / old-fashioned
- simple / sophisticated

Number 3 is a beautiful black modern mobile phone.

The black mobile must be more expensive than the silver one.

Lesson 2

Adverbs of Manner, Place, Time & Degree & Comparison of Adverbs

Adverbs of manner, place, time & degree

Adverbs of manner (slowly, easily, quickly, nicely, etc) tell us how something happens. They answer the question **How ...?** They are often formed by adding **-ly** to adjectives.
Our drama teacher sings *beautifully.*

Adverbs of place (here, there, inside, outside, opposite, in the cinema, etc) tell us where something happens. They answer the question **Where ...?**
Where is the boutique?
The boutique is *over there.*

Adverbs of time (yesterday, today, tomorrow, later, last year, now, etc) tell us when something happens. They answer the question **When ...?**
When are you going to the fashion show?
We are going to the fashion show *tomorrow evening.*

Adverbs of degree (enough, quite, rather, too, so, very, extremely, etc) tell us **how much** or **how many** there is of something or the extent of something.

- adverb + **enough** + full infinitive
  She can't sing *well enough* to become a singer.
- **quite** + adverb
  Alex runs *quite fast.*
- **rather** + adverb
  It's *rather late.*
- **too** + adverb + full infinitive
  We arrived at the play *too late to see* the opening act.

- **so** + adverb
  I didn't realise you spoke Italian *so well.*
- **very/really** + adverb
  You dance *really gracefully*!
- **extremely** + adverb
  You did *extremely well* in the exams.

Note that when we have two or more adverbs in a sentence, they usually come in the following order:
VERB + manner, place, time
Mum *looked quickly around the shop this morning.*

However, when there are verbs in the sentence that show movement, (**come, go, leave, arrive,** etc) the order is:
VERB + place, manner, time
Nicola *arrived at the theatre by car at half past six.*

Some **adverbs of manner** can go before or after the main verb, or at the end of a sentence.
John *quickly* walked out of the room.
John walked *quickly* out of the room.
John walked out of the room *quickly.*

1 Identify the type of adverb in bold.

1. People can be **so** rude sometimes. — _degree_
2. I'm so happy because my grandparent arrived **yesterday**. — _____
3. The book I've just read was **quite** boring. — _____
4. Whenever we have a maths test, Jason finishes **early**. — _____
5. It's too **late** to go to the supermarket now. — _____
6. Lynda runs extremely **fast**. I'm sure she'll win the race. — _____
7. You told me to put the bags over **there**. — _____
8. I love sitting **outside** when it's a nice day. — _____

2 Look at the pictures and complete the sentences. Use these words.

in   ~~here~~   inside   opposite   outside   there

1. Robbie left his guitar _here_ and now it's gone!
2. Due to heavy rain, the concert will take place _____.
3. There the chemist's. It's on the _____ side of the road.
4. Josh is waiting _____ the fish and chip shop.
5. Why are you sitting over _____ on your own?
6. Joanne opened the door and walked _____.

3 Rewrite the sentences, putting the adverbs in brackets in the correct place. Sometimes more than one answer is possible.

1. Marcus waited outside the head teacher's office. (nervously)
   Marcus (nervously) waited (nervously) outside the head teacher's office (nervously).
2. The gold medalist's father stood beside his son. (proudly)
3. Jodie crossed the road. (hurriedly)
4. The band members walked out of the audition. (quietly)
5. When the bell rang, the school children ran outside to play. (happily)
6. Dad agreed to sing at the wedding reception tomorrow evening. (willingly)
7. The school girl gave up her seat on the bus. (reluctantly)
8. My cousin looked at my new silver earrings. (enviously)

4 Write the words in the correct order to make sentences.

1 absolutely / I'm / by / fascinated / folk music
   I'm absolutely fascinated by folk music.

2 has always / lyre / she / extremely / played / the / well

3 Elena / to school / rather / walked / quickly

4 so / speaks / Marcus / Spanish / well

5 too / you / dangerously / live

6 happily / in the park / the children / this morning / ran

7 fast / doesn't drive / Samantha / enough

8 the question / read / please / carefully

9 to go / too / it's / early / to bed

10 waited / impatiently / yesterday afternoon / I / in front of the school gates

---

Comparison of Adverbs

When an adverb has the same form as the adjective, we usually add **–er** to make the comparative and **–est** to make the superlative.

early	earlier	the earliest
fast	faster	the fastest
hard	harder	the hardest
high	higher	the highest
late	later	the latest

When an adverb ends in **–ly**, we use **more/less** to make the comparative form and **the most/the least** to make the superlative form.

beautifully	more/less beautifully	the most/the least beautifully
loudly	more/less loudly	the most/the least loudly

Some adverbs have irregular comparative and superlative forms.

badly	worse	the worst
far	farther/further	the farthest/the furthest
little	less	the least
much	more	the most
well	better	the best

---

5 Complete the sentences with the comparative or superlative form. Use the adverbs in brackets.

1 Sandra takes her singing lessons _less/more seriously than_ Elisa. (seriously)
2 Henry works _____ of all the employees. (fast)
3 Isabel behaved _____ I had expected. (badly)
4 The band played the drums _____ we could imagine! (noisily)
5 Who played the violin _____ in class? (well)
6 You all danced well, however Julie danced _____ . (gracefully)
7 Mrs Harris always explains things _____ Mr Daniels. (clearly)
8 The three sisters speak German well but Olivia speaks it _____ of all. (fluently)

6 Circle the correct words.

1   The musicians noisily were busking / (were busking noisily) in the street.
2   The technician angrily agreed / agreed angry to do a sound check.
3   Frank trained much hardly / harder than we had anticipated for the tennis final.
4   I'm so / too glad you are able to join us!
5   Dad finds jazz music extremely / enough inspiring.
6   We genuinely forgot / forgot genuinely about the dress rehearsal.
7   Carly eats the least healthily / less healthily than her brother.
8   I believe our chemistry teacher communicates with us the most effectively / more effectively.

7 The words in bold are wrong. Write the correct words.

1   Brian is really talented and draws **beautiful**.   _beautifully_
2   I studied hard for the exams and I did very **good**.   _____
3   Josh doesn't run as **faster** as Peter.   _____
4   Please give me a lift because it's raining **inside**.   _____
5   We won't go to the beach today as it's **cold quite**.   _____
6   Ben and Mike tidied their bedroom **quicker** this morning.   _____
7   Don't **loudly speak** in the library.   _____
8   I'm **to** tired to go out tonight.   _____
9   I don't want any more pizza. I've had **absolutely** to eat.   _____
10 My sister solves crossword puzzles **the most** easily than me.   _____

Speaking

Imagine you are a children's TV programme presenter. Talk with your partner about what instructions you would give them to make jelly with fruit and other simple recipes. Use adverbs and these suggestions to help you.

- cut fruit
- boil water
- put powder in bowl
- add boiled water
- stir until powder has melted
- pour into small bowls
- put in fridge
- take jelly out of the fridge

- carefully
- slowly
- completely
- then
- later
- for five hours

You have to cut the fruit carefully.

Then boil the water.

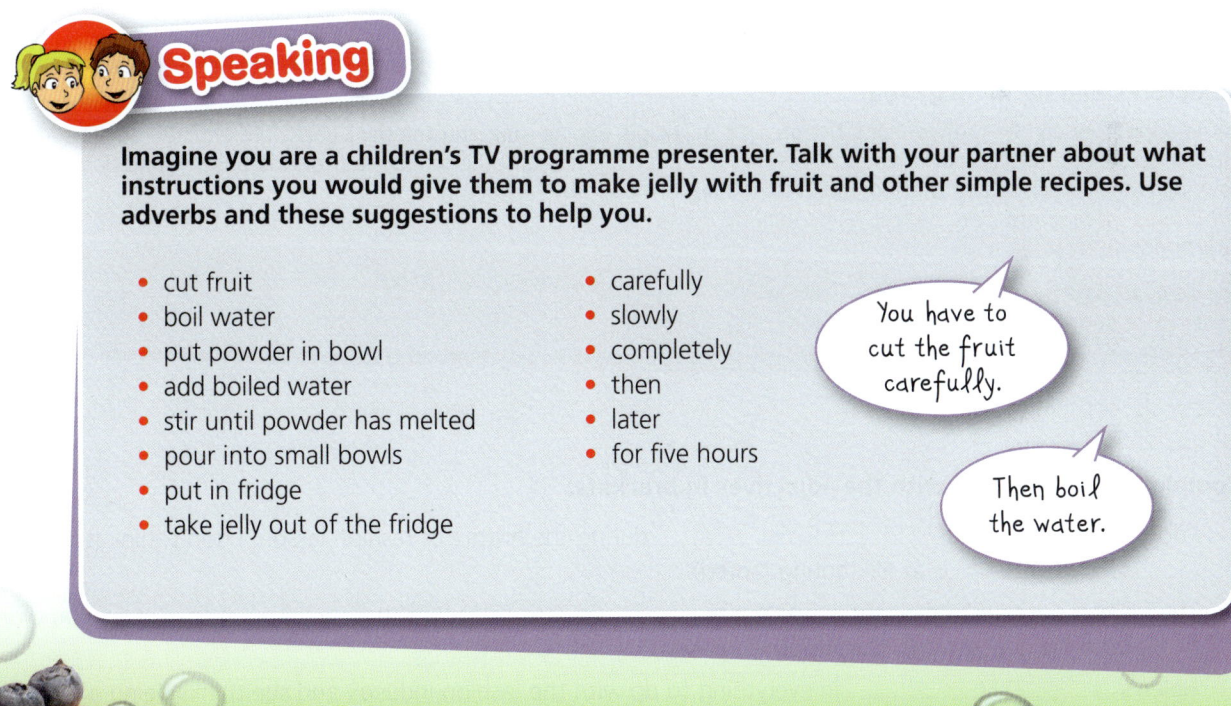

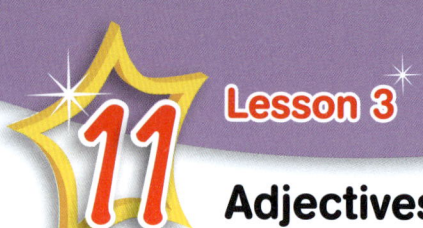

Lesson 3

Adjectives ending in –ing/-ed, Adjectives & Infinitives

Adjectives ending in –ing/-ed
Some adjectives can be formed using the present participle ending **–ing** and the past participle ending **–ed**. The **–ing** form is active and describes the effect someone or something has on others. The **–ed** form is passive and describes how someone or something is affected by something or how they feel about it.
I'm *interested* in sports.
Sports are *interesting*.

The seminar was *motivating*.
I felt *motivated* during the seminar.

1 **Complete the sentences with the adjectives in brackets.**

1. I don't know why you're ____*bored*____ during the history of fashion lesson. I don't think it's ____*boring*____ at all. (boring, bored)
2. The fashion designer's latest show was quite _____ . I'm _____ you didn't hear about his new designs. (surprising, surprised)
3. Helen's _____ in everything to do with the fashion industry and she thinks being a model must be an _____ job. (interesting, interested)
4. I was really _____ when I heard the fire alarm ringing. It was one of the most _____ experiences I've ever had. (frightening, frightened)
5. John's teacher was _____ by his designs. He actually said, 'They are simply _____ !' (amazing, amazed)
6. The film we saw last night was _____ . I was so _____ that I closed my eyes. (terrifying, terrified)

2 Circle the correct words.

1. I find classical music extremely bored / **boring**.
2. Joe was flattered / flattering when the band members asked him to sing with them.
3. Visiting Stonehenge was a fascinated / fascinating experience for me.
4. Elizabeth's job is very fulfilled / fulfilling.
5. Margo's account of why she arrived late wasn't very convinced / convincing.
6. When I do yoga, I feel extremely relaxed / relaxing.
7. Falling down the cliff was a horrified / horrifying experience.
8. Aren't you disappointed / disappointing that your best friend forgot your birthday?

3 Complete the sentences with the correct form of adjectives formed from the words in brackets.

1. Taking part in the concert was the most _____amazing_____ experience ever! (amaze)
2. We were _____ to hear that Susie wanted to give up singing lessons. (surprise)
3. Harry has been feeling very _____ these days. (depress)
4. The conductor looked very _____ . (confuse)
5. The musicians weren't _____ in our demo CD. (interest)
6. I've been practising all day and now I'm _____ . (exhaust)
7. Mainstream fashion is so _____ . (bore)
8. The story of the orphan's childhood was very _____ . (move)

4 Complete the sentences with the correct form of adjectives formed from these verbs.

| alarm | amuse | annoy | confuse | depress | stimulate | tire | worry |

1. It's _____alarming_____ how thin models on the catwalk are.
2. My dog hasn't been eating lately and I'm _____ about him.
3. Training on a daily basis is very _____ .
4. Marcus is bored. He needs a more _____ job.
5. Stop repeating whatever I say! It's so _____ .
6. Ian has lost his DSi and he feels really _____ .
7. I really don't understand. I'm truly _____ .
8. Stop laughing. It really isn't at all _____ .

Adjectives & Infinitives
Adjectives can often be followed by the full infinitive. Sometimes there is an object or a noun after the adjective.

Lizzy is always *happy to lend* Sally her denim jacket.
Making your own evening dress is a *great way to save money*!

5 Write the words in the correct order to make sentences.

1. my homework / willing / me / is / with / to / Matthew / help
   <u>Matthew is willing to help me with my homework.</u>

2. to / a / idea / wear / clothes / it's / a job interview / smart / to / good

3. glad / is / my / progress / maths / to / in / my / teacher / see

4. a / way / pilates / release / fantastic / stress / is / to

5. to / was / her promotion / Melissa / announce / proud

6. activity / is / tiring / gardening / a / very

7. the / to / delighted / hear / I / news / was / good

8. movie / is / great / watch / Finding Nemo / to / a

Speaking

Talk with your partner and exchange opinions about these things. Practise using some of the adjectives you have learnt.

- shopping
- playing computer games
- swimming
- hiking
- watching comedies
- learning a foreign language
- doing your homework

Shopping is boring.

I get bored when I go shopping!

Lesson 1

Pronouns: Reflexive, Indefinite & Possessive

Reflexive Pronouns

We use **reflexive pronouns**
- when the subject and the object of the sentence are the same.
  I gave *myself* a year to get used to life in the city.
- with some verbs (**behave, blame, cut, enjoy, help, hurt,** etc).
  You shouldn't blame *yourself* for the team's defeat.
- when we want to say that somebody does something alone or without somebody else's help. We often use the word **by**.
  We managed to cook dinner by *ourselves*.

Singular	Plural
myself	ourselves
yourself	yourselves
himself	themselves
herself	
itself	

1 Complete the sentences with reflexive pronouns.

1. Mr Henry introduced ____himself____ to the students.
2. My mum sometimes talks to _____ when she is stressed.
3. Sally, did you make all this food by _____?
4. I shouldn't blame _____ for the robbery, but I can't help it.
5. My sister and I injured _____ during the hike.
6. Cats lick _____ to keep clean.
7. I painted my bedroom all by _____ .
8. Our school band members see _____ as professional musicians.

143

Indefinite Pronouns

An **indefinite pronoun** refers to one or more unspecified beings, things or places.

We use **somebody, someone** and **something** to talk about a person or thing in affirmative sentences.
Someone rang me late last night.

We use **anybody, anyone** and **anything** to talk about a person or thing in negative and interrogative sentences.
I can't see anything without my glasses.
Is there anyone at home?

We use **everybody, everyone** and **everything** to talk about all people or things. They are used in the singular form.
Everybody is enjoying the party.

We use **nobody, no one** and **nothing** to talk about no person or thing. They have a negative meaning.
Nobody likes my cooking!

2 Complete the dialogue. Use these words.

anyone   ~~anything~~   everybody   everything   nobody   nothing   someone   something

Amanda: Ross, do you know (1) _anything_ about the Lost City of Atlantis? You're very interested in Greek mythology and the ancient world, so you must know (2) _____ .

Ross: OK, I'll tell you (3) _____ I know. First of all, Atlantis means the 'island of Atlas'. Atlas was a mythological character who supported the world on his shoulders. Plato wrote about Atlantis in about 350 BC. He claimed that it was a beautiful island and that it was located in front of the Pillars of Hercules, which are at the entrance to the Strait of Gibralter. Plato went on to say that Atlantis sank in one day and one night.

Amanda: Does (4) _____ know how it sank?

Ross: Well, once again, Plato claimed that when Atlantis unsuccessfully tried to conquer Athens, it disappeared.

Amanda: (5) _____ must know the truth, though.

Ross: In antiquity, (6) _____ discussed its existence, but few people actually believed it was fact and not fiction.

Amanda: I see. Is it true that (7) _____ has ever found the lost city?

Ross: Yes, it is. In fact, there is (8) _____ to prove that it was real, however the legend of Atlantis continues to inspire writers and film producers.

Possessive pronouns

We use **possessive pronouns** to show that something belongs to someone.
These gloves are mine.

Possessive pronouns replace the possessive adjective and the noun.
This is your pencil. It's yours.

Note that we don't use **its** as a possessive pronoun.

Singular	Plural
mine	ours
yours	yours
his	theirs
hers	
–	

3 Complete the sentences with the correct possessive pronouns.

1 Valery didn't take a hat so I lent her one of _____mine_____ .
2 I am going to bring my CD player. Dennis doesn't need to bring _____ .
3 Warren, are all these computer games _____ ?
4 I don't have a red bag. It can't be _____ .
5 Since you forgot your mobile, ask Kelly if you can use _____ .
6 You don't have to take you car. We are going to take _____ .
7 My next-door neighbours don't like dogs. The puppy in their garden can't be _____ .
8 Children, are these projects _____ ?

4 Choose the correct answers.

1 They want to redecorate their apartment by _____ .
   a) themselves
   b somebody
   c theirs

2 Do you have _____ to donate to the charity?
   a anything
   b something
   c everything

3 There are enough drinks for _____ .
   a no one
   b someone
   c everyone

4 Are these dictionaries _____ ?
   a yourself
   b everyone
   c anybody's

5 Hannah cut _____ while she was chopping up tomatoes.
   a ourselves
   b myself
   c herself

6 We normally do the gardening _____ .
   a ourselves
   b themselves
   c itself

7 I burnt _____ while I was taking the soufflé out of the oven.
   a me
   b mine
   c myself

8 The archaeologists said that the finds were _____ .
   a everyone
   b theirs
   c no one

9 I can't see _____ through this magnifying glass!
   a nothing
   b everything
   c anything

10 Mike can't use _____ laptop because it has a virus.
   a anyone
   b his
   c himself

11 _____ had a wonderful time at he party. All the children went home happy.
   a Nobody
   b Somebody
   c Everybody

12 I have my own room. It's all _____ .
   a ours
   b mine
   c his

145

5 Complete the second sentences so they are similar in meaning to the first sentences. Use the words in bold.

1. Does this laptop belong to you or is it Helen's? **yours**
   Is ___this laptop yours___ or is it Helen's?
2. The bracelet on the dressing table belongs to me. **is**
   The bracelet on the dressing table _____.
3. I didn't have any help making this necklace. **by**
   I made this necklace _____.
4. Joanna can't see anything without her glasses. **can**
   Joanna _____ without her glasses.
5. I can't believe that David made this model plane. **himself**
   I can't believe that David made this _____.
6. There isn't anything on the menu that I can order. **is**
   There _____ that I can order.
7. Mr and Mrs Marsden, take some cake, it's delicious. **help**
   Mr and Mrs Marsden, _____, it's delicious.
8. Our grandmother gave us this priceless jewellery. **is**
   This priceless jewellery _____ now.

Speaking

Imagine that you have made some of these things and that some of these things belong to you. Talk to your partner about them.

It's my school bag. It's mine.

I made the cake by myself.

Lesson 2
Review of Tenses

Review of Tenses
Present Tenses:
Present Simple

We use the **Present Simple** to talk about
- general truths.
- things that we do regularly.
- permanent situations.
- timetabled and programmed events in the future.

I often watch documentaries.
I don't usually have breakfast in the morning.
Do you walk to school every day?
Yes, I do. / No, I don't.

Present Continuous

We use the **Present Continuous** to talk about
- actions that are in progress at the time or around the time of speaking.
- actions that are temporary.
- future plans that we have arranged and they usually refer to the near future.
- annoying habits (with **always, constantly and forever**).
- changing situations.
- what is happening in a picture or photograph.

Right now, we're exploring this unusual site.
They aren't using the laptop at the moment.
Are you talking to me?
Yes, I am. / No, I'm not.

Present Perfect Simple

We use the **Present Perfect Simple** to talk about something that
- started in the past but hasn't finished.
- has just finished.
- happened in the past but we don't know or we don't say exactly when.
- happened in the past but that affects the present.

Daniel has been to Peru twice.
We haven't met our new teacher yet.
Have you ever tried sushi?
Yes, I have. / No, I haven't.

Present Perfect Continuous

We use the **Present Perfect Continuous** to talk about
- something that started in the past and is still in progress.
- something that started in the past and has happened repeatedly.
- something that happened in the past and may have finished, but it has a result in the present.
- how long something has been happening from the past up till now.

My cousins have been living in Dubai for two years.
Dad hasn't been travelling much lately.
Have you been revising since this morning?
Yes, I have. / No, I haven't.

1 Complete the sentences with a correct present tense. Use the words in brackets.

1. Right now, we _____are riding_____ camels in the desert. (ride)
2. I _____ around this museum for three hours! (walk)
3. I _____ my best friend tonight. (not meet)
4. The inhabitants _____ the modern building in the town centre. (not like)
5. The express bus to the centre _____ every hour on the hour. (leave)
6. Aaagh! I _____ a bat before! (never see)
7. We _____ over the Alps at the moment and the view is great! (fly)
8. The sculptor _____ on this statue for six months. (work)
9. _____ a haunted castle? (ever you / visit)
10. The housekeeper _____ the bathroom on a daily basis. (clean)

Past Tenses:
Past Simple

We use the **Past Simple** to talk about
- actions that started and finished in the past.
- past habits.
- actions that happened one after the other in the past.

The archaeologists finished their research three days ago.
Mike didn't score a goal in last night's match.
Did you play with your friends after school?
Yes, I did. / No, I didn't.

Past Continuous

We use the **Past Continuous** to
- talk about an action that was in progress at a specific time in the past.
- talk about two or more actions that were in progress at the same time in the past. We use **and** or **while** to connect the actions.
- describe the scene of a story.
- talk about an action in progress in the past that was interrupted by another action.

At eight o'clock yesterday evening, we were walking home from tennis practice.
Danielle wasn't surfing the Internet while I was studying.
Were you watching the reality show when I called you?
Yes, I was. / No, I wasn't.

Past Perfect Simple

We use the **Past Perfect Simple** to talk about
- something that happened in the past before another action in the past.
- something that happened before a specific time in the past. We often use the word **by** to mean *before* or *not later than*.
- something that happened in the past and had an effect on a later action.

We had never been to such a good concert!
I hadn't finished my homework by the time I went to bed.
Had you visited Paris before you went to live there?
Yes, I had. / No, I hadn't.

Past Perfect Continuous

We use the **Past Perfect Continuous** to
- emphasise the duration of an action that was in progress before another action or time in the past.
- talk about an action that was in progress in the past, which affected a later action or state.

Marcia had been training hard all day so she was exhausted in the evening.
Unfortunately, I hadn't been paying attention during the history lesson!
Had Tony been reading about the mysterious disappearance?
Yes, he had. / No, he hadn't.

2 Circle the correct words.

1 The police were trying / **had been trying** to solve the mystery for a whole year before they found a major clue.
2 Rob was cooking / cooked Veal Parmigiana when I called him last night.
3 While I got / was getting on the bus someone grabbed my handbag.
4 Mark got sunburn as he sat / had been sitting in the sun all morning.
5 Before I went to Milan, I had never seen / didn't see such beautiful boutiques.
6 When she was a teenager, Alice always wore / was always wearing baggy jeans and a T-shirt.
7 While Nicola was walking around the store, she had come across / came across the most stylish bag.
8 The music lesson had already started / already started when Susie walked in.

Future Tenses:
Future Simple

We use the **Future Simple**
- to make predictions.
- to talk about decisions we make at the time of speaking.
- to make offers, promises, threats or to give warnings.
- to ask someone to do something for us.
- to state opinions about the future after **think**, **hope**, **be sure**, **believe**, **bet** and **probably**.

I promise I'll help you find a solution.
We won't tell anyone, don't worry.
Will you take the dog for a walk for me, please?
Yes, I will. / No, I won't.

Be going to

We use **be going to**
- to talk about future plans and intentions.
- to predict that something is going to happen when we have proof or information.

We are going to do many things this weekend.
They aren't going to go to the fashion show.
Are you going to buy that silk scarf?
Yes, I am. / No, I'm not.

149

Future Continuous

We use the **Future Continuous**
- to talk about something that will be in progress at a specific time in the future.
- to ask politely about someone's future plans.

In a month's time, I'll be studying at Oxford University.
Sandra won't be joining us on the hike this weekend.
Will Manuela be working in her father's company this time next year?
Yes, she will. / No, she won't.

Future Perfect Simple

We use the **Future Perfect Simple** to talk about something that will have finished
- before something else happens.
- before a specific time in the future.

By tomorrow night we'll have arrived home.
The film won't have finished by eight o'clock.
Will they have left by the time I get home?
Yes, they will. / No, they won't.

Future Perfect Continuous

We use the **Future Perfect Continuous** to emphasise the duration of an activity that will be in progress before another time or event in the future.

Next month, we'll have been studying Spanish for a year!
I broke my leg and soon, I won't have been playing basketball for a month!
Will you have been teaching for twenty years next year?
Yes, I will. / No, I won't.

Note that we can use the **Present Simple** and the **Present Continuous** to talk about the future.

Present Simple

We use the **Present Simple** to talk about timetabled and programmed events in the future.
The ferry to the island departs at 8 o'clock in the evening.
The school year doesn't start in September in Australia.
Does the flight from Los Angeles arrive at midnight?
Yes, it does. / No, it doesn't.

Present Continuous

We use the **Present Continuous** to talk about fixed future plans.
Sam is going out for dinner after work tonight.
We aren't flying to Madrid tomorrow.
Is Alexander going to the party?
Yes, he is. / No, he isn't.

3 Complete the sentences with the correct future tense. Use these verbs.

buy   depart   do   ~~explore~~   give   meet   start   study

1 This time next month, Joe and I _____will be exploring_____ South America.
2 Amanda believes she _____ well in her music exams.
3 We must be at the airport by six as our flight to Canada _____ at eight o'clock.
4 Don't worry, I _____ you a lift to the theatre.
5 Hopefully, by this time tomorrow we _____ tickets for the rock festival.
6 In a week's time, you _____ Spanish for a year!
7 The school year _____ at the beginning of September in the UK.
8 _____ you _____ Maggie after work tonight?

4 Choose the correct answers.

1. This time tomorrow, I _____ my project about Egypt.
   a have finished
   b **will be finishing** ✓
   c will finish

2. The ferry to Calais _____ at six thirty in the morning.
   a was departing
   b will have been departing
   c departs

3. Mum _____ a huge fan of classical music since she started studying music at school.
   a was
   b had been
   c has been

4. _____ your history project by the end of the week?
   a Will you have finished
   b We you have finished
   c Did you finish

5. Right now, the Eccleston family _____ in Cairo.
   a will have lived
   b is living
   c have been living

6. Alexander Graham Bell _____ the telephone.
   a invented
   b is inventing
   c will have invented

7. By nine o'clock tonight, we _____ this documentary for two hours!
   a will have been watching
   b are watching
   c will be watching

8. While the divers _____ for treasure, they had an accident.
   a looked
   b had looked
   c were looking

9. Not many people _____ in supernatural powers nowadays.
   a have believed
   b believe
   c will believe

10. We arrived at the port after the cruise ship _____ .
    a has left
    b is leaving
    c had left

11. Don't get up. I _____ you a cup of coffee.
    a am going to get
    b has got
    c will get

12. I'm so tired. We _____ the house for hours.
    a have been cleaning
    b are cleaning
    c will be cleaning

5 Complete the article with the correct tense. Use the verbs in brackets.

The Bermuda Triangle

The Bermuda Triangle is also known as the 'Devil's Triangle'. It is a region between Miami, Bermuda and Puerto Rico. Although many years (1) _have passed_ (pass) since the first disappearance, the Bermuda Triangle (2) _____ (be) still a mystery.

For many years now, planes, vessels and people (3) _____ (disappear) in this area, however many ships and aircraft continue to (4) _____ (cross) the triangle on a daily basis. One of the many unusual disappearances is the USS Cyclops, which (5) _____ (depart) from Barbados in March, 1918 and nobody (6) _____ (see) it since.

Some people (7) _____ (believe) the unusual disappearances are caused by supernatural forces. However, researchers (8) _____ (not agree).

Whatever the cause, the Bermuda Triangle (9) _____ (be) a topic of discussion for many years to come and in 100 years' time, people (10) _____ (still try) to solve the mystery.

6 Complete the second sentences so they have a similar meaning to the first sentences. Use the words in bold.

1. Jude started studying astronomy six years ago. **been**
   Jude _has been studying astronomy for_ six years.
2. They are going to visit their grandparents this weekend. **visiting**
   They _____ their grandparents this weekend.
3. Emily is still looking for her ring. **found**
   Emily _____ yet.
4. I plan to finish my novel by next year. **have**
   I _____ my novel by next year.
5. Dad made a coffee and then read the newspaper. **after**
   Dad _____ he had made a coffee.
6. I've been staying with my best friend since Monday. **have**
   I _____ with my best friend for five days by Saturday.
7. I think it will be a nice day tomorrow. **rain**
   I _____ tomorrow.
8. This is the first time Maria has written a novel. **never**
   Maria _____ a novel before.
9. My sister and I always have breakfast and then we go to school. **before**
   My sister and I _____ we go to school.
10. Carla fell asleep on the beach. Then, she came out in a rash. **had**
    After Carla _____ on the beach, she came out in a rash.

Speaking

Talk with your partner about how these things were in the past, how they are now and how you think they'll be in the future. Use these suggestions to help you. Use the appropriate tenses.

- transport
- education
- heating
- cooking
- housing
- free time
- leisure activities
- communication

In the past, most people walked to wherever they needed to go to.

Nowadays, a lot of people take the bus or the train to reach where they want to go to.

Lesson 3
So & Such

So & Such

We use **so** and **such** to give emphasis.

so + adjective
The Temple of Poseidon in Sounion is so beautiful.

so + adverb
The baby cried so loudly when it fell out of its pram.

so + **much/many** + noun
There are so many archaeological sites in Sicily.

such + (a/an) + adjective + noun
We had such an amazing time at the funfair.

such + noun
The expedition was such a success.

Note that we can replace **such** + **a/an** + adjective + noun with **so** + adjective + **a/an** + noun.
It was such a strange place that I felt scared.
It was so strange a place that I felt scared.

1 Complete the sentences with **so** or **such**.

1 It was ____so____ incredibly hot in the desert that we couldn't even walk.
2 Marilyn is _____ a stylish model.
3 He was _____ persuasive a person that we bought the house without thinking twice!
4 Lilly is _____ a wonderful dancer.
5 I can't believe you are _____ superficial.
6 The Loch Ness Monster is still _____ a mystery.
7 Mandy has _____ many computer games.
8 The works of Gaudi are _____ unusual.

2 Choose the correct words.

1 100 euros for a pair of shoes! I can't believe they're _____ .
   - (a) so expensive
   - b such expensive
   - c such an expensive

2 It was _____ last night that I couldn't sleep.
   - a such a hot
   - b so hot a
   - c so hot

3 Kelly is _____ girl!
   - a so clever
   - b such a clever
   - c clever

4 It was _____ train, it went from Melbourne to Sydney in only six hours.
   - a so fast
   - b such a fast
   - c fast

5 We aren't going to the cinema tonight. We have got _____ homework to do.
   - a such
   - b so much
   - c so many

6 Josh and Melinda are _____ children!
   - a so noisy
   - b such noisy
   - c such a noisy

7 How could you say _____ thing to your mother?
   - a awful
   - b such an awful
   - c so awful

8 I can't believe that Peter lied to his parents. He is _____ a boy.
   - a so good
   - b such a good
   - c such good

3 Complete the sentences with so (a/ an), such (a/ an), or and these words.

| cheap | efficient | ~~frightening~~ | fun | heavy | high | intelligent | waste |

1 The film was _so frightening_ that the viewers couldn't watch it!
2 Melanie is _____ employee that she's always given bonuses.
3 The rain was _____ that the match was postponed.
4 We had _____ at the funfair that we didn't stop laughing.
5 It was _____ mountain that the climber couldn't reach the top.
6 The designer clothes were _____ in the sales that I bought lots of new dresses.
7 The professor is _____ person.
8 The meeting was _____ of time.

4 Circle the correct words.

1 The music is (so)/such loud! I wish they would turn it down.
2 She spoke so quickly / quickly that I couldn't understand what she was saying.
3 The investigation was such / so a disaster.
4 I can't believe that the furniture is such / so expensive.
5 It was such a luxurious / so luxurious hotel that I didn't want to leave.
6 The children had so enjoyable / such an enjoyable time at the party.

5 Complete the second sentences so they have a similar meaning to the first sentences. Use the words in bold.

1. My day was so busy that I didn't have time to have lunch. **such**
   I had _____such a busy day that_____ I didn't have time to have lunch.
2. Sardinia has got such nice beaches we are thinking of going back next year. **nice**
   The beaches in Sardinia _____ we are thinking of going back next year.
3. The book about UFOs was so fascinating I couldn't put it down! **a**
   It was _____ that I couldn't put it down.
4. It was such a boring presentation that some of the participants fell asleep. **was**
   The presentation _____ that some of the participants fell asleep.
5. The journey was so incredible that I'd like to go on a similar one again. **an**
   It was _____ that I'd like to go on a similar one again.
6. Hannah spoke to the head teacher in such a rude way that she was given a detention. **so**
   Hannah spoke to _____ that she was given a detention.
7. The comedy was so funny that I couldn't stop laughing. **a**
   It was _____ that I couldn't stop laughing.
8. Pilates is such a relaxing activity that I've decided to practise it regularly. **so**
   Pilates is _____ that I've decided to practise it regularly.

Talk to you partner about these things. Use so, such and the suggestions to help you.

- best friend
- homework
- holiday
- music shop
- brother
- TV programme

- character
- appearance
- exciting
- boring
- CDs
- naughty

Katie is my best friend. She's such a nice person.

I've got so much homework tonight.

Units 11 & 12

1 Put the adjectives in brackets in the correct order and complete the sentences.

1 Helen bought me some ___nice black leather___ gloves. (leather / black / nice)
2 Who made that _____ statue? (grey / awful / old)
3 My cousins stayed in a _____ cottage. (little / white / stunning)
4 Delia was wearing a(n) _____ hat at the fashion show last night. (straw / big / unusual)
5 Have you seen my _____ purse? (velvet / tiny / green)
6 I'm going to buy that _____ watch later on today. (silver / gorgeous / Swiss)

2 Choose the correct answers.

1 The weather is getting _____ year by year.
  a) warmer
  b the warmest
  c warmest

2 Are diamonds _____ than pearls?
  a the most expensive
  b more expensive
  c as expensive as

3 I arrived at the temple _____ than you.
  a the earliest
  b early
  c earlier

4 Thomas speaks English _____ of all the students in the class.
  a the least fluently
  b less fluently
  c as fluently as

5 Unfortunately, we weren't _____ as we had thought.
  a the best prepared
  b better prepared
  c as well prepared

6 What is _____ thing in the world?
  a most important
  b the most important
  c as important as

7 In my opinion, solar power is _____ wind power.
  a more efficient
  b as efficient as
  c the most efficient

8 I find cross country racing _____ .
  a challenged
  b challenging
  c challenge

9 The more I read about extra terrestrials, _____ I want to learn about space.
  a more than
  b the more
  c the most

10 I am quite _____ by the number of disappearances in the area.
  a to disturb
  b disturbed
  c disturbing

3 Complete the sentences. Use these words.

| enough | excitedly | later | ~~outside~~ | so | yesterday |

1 It's a beautiful day today. Let's have lunch ___outside___ .
2 Tamara walked into the oral exam _____ confidently.
3 I feel better today than I did _____ .
4 Will they be dropping in _____ on today?
5 The children waved _____ at Mickey Mouse.
6 I can't act well _____ to become an actor.

4 Complete the sentences with adjectives ending in –ing or –ed formed from the words in brackets.

1. I was so _____frightened_____ that I couldn't sleep. (frighten)
2. Running cross country is very _____ . (tire)
3. The film was so _____ that I couldn't keep my eyes open. (bore)
4. The children really enjoyed the performance. They were thoroughly _____ . (amuse)
5. The actor felt _____ when he forgot his words. (embarrass)
6. I think learning about other cultures is really _____ . (interest)
7. I love going on rollercoaster rides. It's _____ . (excite)
8. Lyn was _____ to hear the good news. (thrill)

5 The words in bold are wrong. Write the correct words.

1. I'd like **nobody** to tell me the origins of face painting, please.   ___somebody___
2. Are the singers going to write the lyrics by **ourselves**?   _____
3. Is this black leather jacket **your**?   _____
4. There was **anything** interesting in the newspaper so I threw it away.   _____
5. I was really tired because **anybody** helped me with the bags.   _____
6. I was in a haunted castle all by **me**.   _____
7. I don't have black sunglasses. They aren't **my**.   _____
8. Josh wants to decorate his room all by **him**.   _____

6 Complete the dialogue with the correct tense. Use the verbs in brackets.

Nina: Harry, I (1) _____am thinking_____ (think) of writing an article on the Loch Ness Monster. (2) _____ (you / believe) there is any truth in it?
Harry: I (3) _____ (not know).
Nina: Well, the modern myth all started in 1933. A local couple, the Spicers, (4) _____ (drive) along Loch Ness, which is a long narrow deep lake in Scotland, when they (5) _____ (see) a large creature crossing the road in front of them. Since then, people (6) _____ (try) to take pictures of it. It's weird that before 1933, nobody (7) _____ (ever spot) it, isn't it?
Harry: Yes, that's true.
Nina: Anyhow, in 1934, R K Wilson claimed that he (8) _____ (take) a photo of Nessie.
Harry: Nessie?
Nina: Yes, the monster is often referred to as Nessie.
Harry: Mm. Most scientists (9) _____ (believe) that it's a myth, though.
Nina: Yes, they do. However, I (10) _____ (think) in a hundred years' time, people (11) _____ (still investigate) the mystery. So, myth or no myth, for years to come, it (12) _____ (always be) fascinating.

7 Complete the sentences with so or such.

1. Marcia is _____so_____ rude that I can't stand her!
2. You have _____ bad an attitude that you'll never succeed.
3. Mozart was _____ a great composer!
4. You're wearing _____ beautiful cowboy boots.
5. Bagpipes are _____ fascinating!
6. Dad is _____ spontaneous a person, he never plans ahead.

Review 6
Units 11 & 12

Writing Project

1 Look at a project about the Great Pyramid of Giza. Circle the correct words.

A Marvellous Mystery

The (1) huge ancient Egyptian / Egyptian ancient huge Great Pyramid of Giza, which (2) also knows / is also known as the Cheops Pyramid, is the largest of the three pyramids and the oldest of the Seven Wonders of the Ancient World. It (3) used to / is used to be the tallest man-made structure in the world and it remains one of the most (4) fascinated / fascinating in history. However, many details about its construction remain a mystery.

People (5) believe / are believing that the Great Pyramid was built as a tomb for Cheops the Pharaoh, by Cheops' highest official, Hemon, and that construction lasted between 14 and 20 years. However, there is still mystery surrounding its construction. Even today, (6) anybody / nobody is sure of the techniques used to build the pyramid but the theory that huge blocks of limestone (7) have been moved / were moved from a quarry and then put into place is (8) the most convincing / convinced. Even its original height is (9) rather uncertain / uncertain rather. Another mystery is who (10) was the pyramid built / did the pyramid built by? According to the Ancient Greeks, slaves built the pyramid whilst modern Egyptologists (11) insist / are insisting that skilled workers (12) employed / were employed.

2 Now it's your turn to do a project about a mysterious construction. Find or draw a picture of it and write about it.

depressed (adj)
flatter (v)
mainstream (adj)
orphan (n)
promotion (n)
stress (n)

UNIT TWELVE

Lesson One
bracelet (n)
defeat (n)
donate (v)
existence (n)
inspire (v)
legend (n)
magnifying glass (n)
mythological (adj)
necklace (n)
priceless (adj)
souffle (n)

Lesson Two
handbag (n)
haunted (adj)
mysterious (adj)
novel (n)
rash (n)

stylish (adj)
supernatural (adj)
sushi (n)
topic (n)
treasure (n)
Veal Parmigiana (n)
vessel (n)

Lesson Three
investigation (n)
persuasive (adj)
rudely (adv)
superficial (adj)
UFO (n)

REVIEW 6
Egyptologist (n)
extra terrestrials (n)
limestone (n)
lyrics (pl n)
man-made (adj)
origin (n)
quarry (n)
slave (n)
spontaneous (adj)
thoroughly (adv)
velvet (adj)

Lesson Two
calculator (n)
exception (n)
mortgage (n)
overalls (pl n)
repair (v)
traffic warden (n)

Lesson Three
adverse (adj)
assault (v)
casualty (n)
death toll (phr)
discourage (v)
evidence (n)
fence (n)
hit and run (phr)
hooligan (n)
inhabitant (n)
innocent (adj)
open-minded (phr)
optimistic (adj)
prosecute (v)
riot (n)
shoplifting (n)
surveillance camera (n)
vandal (n)
vanilla (adj)

REVIEW 5
bricklayer (n)
cement (n)
consumer (n)
countless (adj)
delicious (adj)
enable (v)
flock (v)
hesitate (v)
lecturer (n)
market research (phr)
mountainous (adj)
population (n)
revise (v)
richter scale (phr)
sample (n)
tremendously (adv)

UNIT ELEVEN

Lesson One
ball gown (n)
boutique (n)
cowboy boots (n)
gorgeous (adj)
linen (adj)
marble (n)
multi-coloured (adj)
old-fashioned (adj)
overtime (n)
pearl (n)
silk (adj)
sophisticated (adj)
statue (n)
straw (adj)
torn (adj)
unique (adj)
wooden (adj)

Lesson Two
busk (v)
dress rehearsal (phr)
enviously (adv)
fluently (adv)
folk music (phr)
gracefully (adv)
hurriedly (adv)
impatiently (adv)
nervously (adv)
proudly (adv)
reluctantly (adv)
sound check (phr)
willingly (adv)

Lesson Three
catwalk (n)
conductor (n)

renovation (n)
solar panel (n)
structure (n)
sunlight (n)
ventilation (n)

UNIT NINE

Lesson One
applicant (n)
assignment (n)
bonus (n)
courier (n)
economise (v)
economist (n)
estate agency (n)
graduation ceremony (phr)
job hunting (phr)
leather (n)
planetarium (n)
recession (n)
redundant (adj)
small business grant (phr)
supportive (adj)
technician (n)
tourism (n)

Lesson Two
botany (n)
careers advisor (n)
cough syrup (n)
enrol (v)
fax machine (n)
filing cabinet (n)
film industry (phr)
film producer (n)
Human Resources Manager (n)
media studies (phr)
peanut butter (n)
postpone (v)
production company (n)
supervisor (n)
swimming instructor (n)

vacancy (n)
wildlife (n)

Lesson Three
accuse (v)
admit (v)
beg (v)
boast (v)
burst (v)
complain (v)
delete (v)
deny (v)
disastrous (adj)
exclaim (v)
impolite (adj)
insist on (phr verb)
photocopying machine (n)
plumber (n)
remark (v)
remind (v)
resignation (n)
suggest (v)

UNIT TEN

Lesson One
aircraft (n)
aquarium (n)
contributor (n)
detect (v)
dormant (adj)
eruption (n)
evacuate (v)
extinguish (v)
gardener (n)
jewellery (n)
lifeguard (n)
purchase (v)
renovate (v)
seismic (adj)
shipwreck (n)
severe (adj)

windmill (n)

Lesson Two
astronomy (n)
bazaar (n)
cinema complex (phr)
graffiti (pl n)
financial crisis (phr)
firewood (n)
hydroelectric power (phr)
marathon (n)
microwave (n)
millionaire (n)
nuclear power station (n)
organic (adj)
projector (n)

Lesson Three
dam (n)
delay (v)
dishwasher (n)
download (v)
eventually (adv)
insult (v)
medicine (n)

UNIT EIGHT

Lesson One
anxious (adj)
ashamed (adj)
doorstep (n)
facebook (n)
glad (adj)
godparent (n)
invitation (n)
lock (v)
make an effort (phr)
voucher (n)
willing (adj)
workman (n)

Lesson Two
compass (n)
consume (v)

data (n)
first aid kit (phr)
fruit salad (n)
GPS (n)
inflate (v)
keyboard (n)
language lab (n)
online (adv)
mall (n)
memory stick (n)
mosquito repellent (n)
petrol (n)
piggy bank (n)
printer (n)
reptile (n)
sunblock (n)
sunstroke (n)
video shop (n)
whistle (n)

Lesson Three
author (n)
award-winning (adj)
cheaply (adv)
interior designer (n)
iPad (n)
redecorate (v)
upgrade (v)
wireless (adj)

REVIEW 4
architectural (adj)
bark (v)
cash card (n)
consumption (n)
environmentally-friendly (phr)
gherkin (n)
impressive (adj)
install (v)
ironing (n)
monitor (n)
presentation (n)

double-decker bus (n)
extinct (adj)
interstate (adj)
knock (v)
moped (n)
slippery (adj)
species (n)

UNIT SIX

Lesson One
aerobics teacher (n)
check-up (phr)
cholesterol (n)
chore (n)
convenience food (phr)
DSi (n)
escalator (n)
interpreter (n)
lettuce (n)
overweight (adj)
sedentary (adj)
spaghetti bolognaise (n)
turn off (phr v)
vacuum (v)

Lesson Two
allergic (adj)
antibiotics (pl n)
art gallery (n)
asthma (n)
calorie (n)
first-aid course (phr)
gluten (n)
immediately (adv)
nutritional (adj)
protein (n)
tooth decay (phr)
watermelon (n)

Lesson Three
accidentally (adv)
digest (v)

lottery (n)
salesman (n)
tasteless (adj)

REVIEW 3
ancient (adj)
biologist (n)
cabin (n)
carbohydrate (n)
catamaran (n)
crossword (n)
experiment (n)
field trip (phr)
household chores (phr)
leisure centre (n)
moderation (n)
MP4 player (n)
research (n)
retake (v)
source (n)
stream (n)
volume (n)
well-being (phr)

UNIT SEVEN

Lesson One
blade (n)
climate change (phr)
drought (n)
efficient (adj)
emit (v)
fossil fuel (phr)
grain (n)
grind (v)
pump (v)
renewable (adj)
satellite (n)
shaft (n)
solar system (phr)
spin (n)
turbine (n)

university (n)

Lesson Three
boarding school (n)
cereal (n)
century (n)
community (n)
explorer (n)
healthily (adv)
historical (adj)
interactive whiteboard (n)
knitting (n)
Latin (adj)
remote (adj)
resident (n)
routine (n)
summer school (n)

REVIEW 1
athlete (n)
boast (v)
citizen (n)
classical music (phr)
collapse (v)
conquer (v)
dinner party (phr)
dominate (v)
empire (n)
fame and fortune (phr)
fashion designer (n)
finish line (phr)
gladiator (n)
guitarist (n)
leaflet (n)
magnificent (adj)
monarchy (n)
olive (n)
proof (n)
republic (n)
secretary (n)
songwriter (n)
underground (n)

vintage (adj)

UNIT THREE
Lesson One
blog (n)
darts competition (n)
forecast (n)
kayaking (n)
raffle ticket (n)
remote control (n)
rival (n)
rounders (n)
scuba diving instructor (n)
seashell (n)
select (v)
Tudor times (phr)
weatherman (n)

Lesson Two
adventurous (adj)
break the world record (phr)
difficulty (n)
diving instructor (n)
flow (v)
handball (n)
kite surfing (n)
literature (n)
milkshake (n)
participate (v)
reckless (adj)
risky (adj)
scholarship (n)
track and field (phr)
trophy (n)
white water rafting (n)

Lesson Three
admire (v)
archery (n)
bungee jumping (n)
contestant (n)
parachuting (n)

professional (adj)
slope (n)
strenuous (adj)
tournament (n)
wildlife (n)
yoga (n)
youth club (n)

UNIT FOUR

Lesson One
ambulance (n)
power cut (n)
pros and cons (phr)
rooftop (n)
stray (adj)
urban (adj)

Lesson Two
assignment (n)
exotic (adj)
peaceful (adj)
relaxing (adj)
security alarm (n)
suburb (n)

Lesson Three
approximately (adv)
architect (n)
blockbuster (adj)
border (n)
eagle (n)
funfair (n)
graduate (n)
hide-and-seek (phr)
homeless (pl n)
lawyer (n)
mythology (n)
national team (phr)
nowadays (adv)
roof garden (phr)
spectacular (adj)
trumpet (n)
violin (n)

REVIEW 2
abroad (adv)
cobbled (adj)
concentration (n)
construct (v)
dull (adj)
endangered (adj)
picturesque (adj)
bicycle lane (n)
botanical gardens (n)
facility (n)
hustle and bustle (phr)
inner city (phr)
mayor (n)
maze (n)
muscle (n)
pilates (n)
praline (n)
outskirts (pl n)
retire (v)
speciality (n)
tarantula (n)
tropical (adj)

UNIT FIVE

Lesson One
atlas (n)
board (v)
cross-country skiing (n)
fingerprint (n)
husky (n)
reindeer (n)
stimulate (v)

Lesson Two
annual (adj)
archaeologist (n)
expedition (n)
fete (n)
iron (v)

Lesson Three
camper van (n)

Irregular verbs

Infinitive	Past Simple	Past participle
be	was/were	been
become	became	become
begin	began	begun
bet	bet	bet
bite	bit	bitten
break	broke	broken
bring	brought	brought
build	built	built
burn	burnt	burnt
buy	bought	bought
catch	caught	caught
choose	chose	chosen
come	came	come
cost	cost	cost
cut	cut	cut
die	died	died
dig	dug	dug
do	did	done
draw	drew	drawn
drink	drank	drunk
drive	drove	driven
eat	ate	eaten
fall	fell	fallen
feed	fed	fed
feel	felt	felt
fight	fought	fought
find	found	found
fly	flew	flown
forget	forgot	forgotten
get	got	got
give	gave	given
go	went	gone
grow	grew	grown
have	had	had
hear	heard	heard
hide	hid	hidden
hit	hit	hit
hold	held	held
hurt	hurt	hurt
keep	kept	kept
know	knew	known

Infinitive	Past Simple	Past participle
learn	learnt	learnt
leave	left	left
lend	lent	lent
let	let	let
lie	lay	lain
lose	lost	lost
make	made	made
mean	meant	meant
meet	met	met
pay	paid	paid
put	put	put
read	read	read
ride	rode	ridden
ring	rang	rung
run	ran	run
say	said	said
see	saw	seen
sell	sold	sold
send	sent	sent
shoot	shot	shot
show	showed	shown
sing	sang	sung
sit	sat	sat
sleep	slept	slept
smell	smelt	smelt
speak	spoke	spoken
spend	spent	spent
stand	stood	stood
steal	stole	stolen
sweep	swept	swept
swim	swam	swum
take	took	taken
teach	taught	taught
tell	told	told
think	thought	thought
throw	threw	thrown
understand	understood	understood
wake	woke	woken
wear	wore	worn
win	won	won
write	wrote	written

Word list

UNIT ONE

Lesson One

apartment (n)
appointment (n)
assignment (n)
audition (v)
celebrity (n)
charity (n)
colleague (n)
constantly (adv)
dentist (n)
depart (v)
forever (adv)
get the chance (phr)
increase (v)
judge (n)
medallist (n)
noodle (n)
publish (v)
raise (v)
rehearse (v)
sculptor (n)
sign (v)

Lesson Two

awful (adj)
comedy (n)
consider (v)
director (n)
fabric (n)
festival (n)
formal (adj)
musical (n)
pub (n)
stardom (n)
track (music) (n)

Lesson Three

candy (n)
carton (n)
diamond (n)
hilarious (adj)
magician (n)
popcorn (n)
poverty-stricken (adj)
telescope (n)
white lie (phr)

UNIT TWO

Lesson One

archaeological (adj)
bump into sb (phr verb)
destination (n)
disaster (n)
documentary (n)
excursion (n)
glimpse (v)
glorious (adj)
iceberg (n)
lifeboat (n)
passenger ship (n)
portrait (n)
pour (v)
PSP (n)
vase (n)
voyage (n)

Lesson Two

(the) aristocracy (n)
battle (n)
bullfighting (n)
championship (n)
cottage (n)
decade (n)
gossip magazine (n)
science fiction books (n)
stunning (adj)